ATLANTA

THE CAMPAIGN FOR

CIVIL WAR SERIES

TEXT BY ALBERT CASTEL

Published by Eastern National, copyright 1996.

Thanks to Bill Scaife, Dennis Kelly, and the interpretive staff at Kennesaw Mountain National Battlefield Park.

Eastern National provides quality educational products and services to
America's national parks and other public trusts.

Cover: *War Is Hell,* by Mort Künstler. Copyright 1991 Mort Künstler, Inc. This painting depicts Sherman
abandoning Atlanta during his March to the Sea.

Back cover: Federal Attack on Kennesaw Mountain, by Thure de Thulstrup.
Courtesy of The Seventh Regiment Fund, Inc.

Maps by Laura Kriegstrom Poracsky from *Decision in the West: The Atlanta Campaign of 1864* by Albert Castel,
courtesy of Mr. Castel and the University Press of Kansas.

Printed on recycled paper.

THE CAMPAIGN FOR ATLANTA

"God help my country!" So wrote Mary Chesnut of South Carolina in her diary on New Year's Day 1864. She expressed the feeling of the vast majority of her fellow Southerners. Their expectation of victory, so high at the beginning of 1863, had by the end of that year been transformed into a dread of impending doom by the disastrous defeats at Gettysburg, Vicksburg, and Chattanooga. Powerful Northern armies now dominated vast areas of the South and stood poised to overrun still more against badly depleted Confederate forces. The South's economy was close to collapse, thousands of its people were homeless refugees, its ramshackle rail system barely functioned, the Northern blockade was growing evermore effective, and any chance that Britain would recognize and aid the Confederacy had disappeared with the Emancipation Proclamation and the failure of Robert E. Lee's second invasion of the North at Gettysburg.

Yet, in spite of all of this, the South retained, as 1864 got under way, one last hope of victory. Paradoxically, this hope came from the North. There the Democratic party contended that the nation never could be reunited by war but only through peace, a peace to be achieved by giving the seceded states an opportunity to return to the Union with the same rights—among them the right of slavery—that they had held when they left it. Accordingly, the Democrats based their strategy, which they made no attempt to conceal, for the North's 1864 presidential election on two assumptions: (1) that notwithstanding their 1863 setbacks the Confederates would be able to defy all efforts to subdue them through the spring, summer, and fall of 1864; (2) that as a consequence war-weary Northern voters, realizing the futility of trying to suppress the rebellion by military means, would repudiate the pro-war and antislavery policies of the Republicans by replacing Abraham Lincoln in the White House with a Democrat pledged to a suspension of hostilities and the negotiation of a voluntary restoration of the Union.

The assumptions of the Democrats gave Southerners their hope of victory in 1864. They believed that if they could hold out long and well enough against the Yankee armies they would break the

MARY CHESNUT

(NA)

will of the North to go on with the war and so open the way for the Democrats to take power in Washington, an event that would lead—not to the South returning to the Union, for it had fought too hard and suffered too much to do that— but rather to Northern acceptance of Southern independence: once the North stopped the war it would be impossible for it to resume it.

What brought hope to Southerners inspired fear among Republicans. They too realized that should the Federal armies be bogged down in stalemate come election time, the North indeed might turn to the Democrats with their specious but seductive promise of Union through peace. To prevent this from happening it would be necessary either to defeat the Confederacy before the voters went to the polls in the fall or else to score such military successes as to convince the majority of those voters that victory was on the way. That was why on February 1, 1864, Lincoln issued a call for 200,000 more troops in addition to the 300,000 he had summoned to the colors in October: these 500,000 new soldiers would be twice the number the Confederacy could muster altogether. It

also was why Lincoln on March 9, 1864, appointed Ulysses S. Grant to the newly created rank of lieutenant general and placed him in command of all Union armies. If Grant, who had captured whole Rebel armies at Fort Donelson and Vicksburg and routed another at Chattanooga, could not lead the North to victory in 1864, who could?

Such, then, were the grand strategies of North and South as the war entered its fourth year. In the case of the South, it sought to win by not losing, in the hope that the North, finding itself unable to win, would lose its will to continue the war. As for the North, Lincoln and the Republicans needed and therefore would endeavor to win by winning, thus main-

taining the support of the Northern people for the war and for themselves. Which strategy prevailed and which failed would be decided on the battlefields.

If the South was to win by not losing, there were two places where it was absolutely essential to deny the North victory: Virginia and Georgia. Confederate President Jefferson Davis was confident that Lee could hold the Yankees at bay in Virginia, preventing them from taking Richmond, the capital of the Confederacy and the symbol of its independence.

He lacked the same confidence in General Joseph E. Johnston, commander of the Confederate Army of Tennessee in north Georgia. He considered Johnston to be vain and selfish as a man and as a general more inclined to retreat than to fight, to defend rather than to attack, and so recalcitrant in implementing the wishes of the government with regard to military operations as to border on the insubordinate. Therefore, he had appointed Johnston to command the Army of Tennessee, following its debacle at Chattanooga in November 1863, most reluctantly and solely because no other general of the requisite rank was available who could be depended on to do better or even as well. He could only hope that Johnston, now that the fate of the Confederacy hung in the balance, would be more cooperative, more aggressive, and above all more successful than he hitherto had been.

It would be a vain hope. Johnston's dislike and distrust of Davis matched, indeed exceeded, the president's dislike and distrust of the general. Johnston knew, too, that Davis had named him to head the Army of Tennessee out of necessity, not preference, and suspected that Davis would not be altogether unhappy should he fail in that post. Accordingly, although he would do his best, by his lights, to defend Georgia, as always he would take care while doing so to preserve his public reputation for high military skill, a reputation that literally was more precious to him than life itself.

How difficult it was for Davis and Johnston to work in harmony became evident from the start. Soon after Johnston took command of the Army of Tennessee at Dalton, Georgia, on December 27, 1863, he received a letter from the president urging him to attack and defeat the Federal army at Chattanooga, thereby forestalling an invasion of Georgia by delivering what in effect would be a preemptive strike. In theory it was a good plan but in fact utterly impracticable. As Johnston promptly and correctly pointed out in reply, the Army of Tennessee lacked the strength, supplies, and transport to conduct a successful offensive. The only way it could reasonably hope to do so, Johnston argued, was to repel the Federals when they attacked, then launch a counterattack. To that end he asked that he be reinforced by Lieutenant General Leonidas Polk's army in Mississippi and Alabama.

Davis, who had received contrary information from other sources, refused to believe Johnston's assessment of the Army of Tennessee's offensive capability. To him it seemed that Johnston was being his

GENESIS IN STEEL:
RAILROADS BUILD A CITY

*M*ore than any other Southern city that flourished before the Civil War, Atlanta was a creation of the railroad. It lay perfectly uninhabited in 1840, when survey crews began marking the location of three rail lines that would connect there. The Georgia Railroad extended from Augusta to the east, while the Macon & Western worked its way up from the south. These lines led into the wilderness from the more populated coast, but a third railroad, the Western & Atlantic, snaked its way south through the mountains from Chattanooga, on the Tennessee border. Engineers opted to join these roads a few miles south of the Chattahoochee River, and they named this arbitrary junction "Terminus." Colonel Stephen Long, the chief engineer of the Western & Atlantic, reportedly refused a chance to buy 200 acres in Terminus because he doubted the place would ever amount to anything.

In 1843 the site was incorporated under the name of Marthasvllle. Two years later its name was changed again, to Atlanta. Colonel Long's disdained 200 acres formed the center of the city, which blossomed rapidly. By 1860 Atlanta could boast a population of more than 10,000, and it was still growing.

The city was recognized early in the war as a vital link in Confederate communications. The Western & Atlantic Railroad, in particular, served as an umbilical between the Upper South and the Deep South, connecting with the equally important rail center at Chattanooga, about 140 miles to the north. As early as April of 1862 Union authorities had attached enough significance to the Western & Atlantic that Federal soldiers infiltrated northern Georgia in civilian clothing and stole a locomotive with the intention of cutting the line. That incursion ended in disaster, as did Union Colonel Abel Streight's cavalry raid in the spring of 1863, which culminated in the capture of Streight's command by Confederate cavalry under General Nathan Bedford Forrest.

The Western & Atlantic proved even more crucial as a supply line as Federal armies pushed the Confederate Army of Tennessee eastward in the summer of 1863. When Union troops occupied Chattanooga and Knoxville that fall, however, they interrupted all rail traffic north of Dalton, Georgia. The Western & Atlantic thereafter ceased to hold its former strategic value for the South: as 1864 opened, the only major rail link between the two major Confederate armies was the overburdened coastal route.

Atlanta itself remained vital to the Confederacy, despite the diminished importance of the Western & Atlantic. The city still served as a terminus for three rail lines that led to the unoccupied portions of the besieged nation, and it rivaled Richmond in its industrial importance to the South. Its railroad heritage had spawned machine shops, mills, and foundries that supplied demands from Mississippi to the Carolinas, and if it were lost those demands would be thrown upon the distant Richmond factories that were already falling behind in production, from which goods would have to be transported hundreds of additional miles over railroads that were already too taxed.

As William Sherman's troops prepared to move south in the spring of 1864, Atlanta had doubled in population as its industrial base expanded to support the machinery of war. Warehouses bulged with matériel for the Army of Tennessee, while trains steamed hourly out of the city to the east, west, and south with military or mechanical provisions and equipment. Meanwhile—just in case—Confederate engineers were putting the finishing touches on a series of artillery redoubts and rifle pits that partially surrounded the city.

—William Marvel

TRAIN SHED IN
ATLANTA.

(LC)

*While
Johnston
and Davis
wrangled,
Grant formu-
lated a plan
for winning
the war for
the North.*

usual uncooperative and unaggressive self. Hence for the next four months he endeavored to persuade Johnston to go after the Yankees before the Yankees came after him. Just as persistently Johnston refused to do anything of the kind. Since Davis, for political reasons, dared not remove Johnston or order him to attack, by default Johnston's strategy for meeting and defeating the Union invasion of Georgia became the Confederate strategy.

While Johnston and Davis wrangled, Grant formulated a plan for winning the war for the North. Basically it called for Grant, who had decided to take personal charge of operations in Virginia, to smash Lee and/or take Richmond, and for the Union forces at Chattanooga to crush Johnston and/or take Atlanta, a vital railroad and manufacturing center with a strategic and symbolic importance second only to that of Richmond. Should either city fall, then it would merely be a matter of time before the Confederacy itself fell—and both Northerners and Southerners realized this.

To conduct the campaign against Johnston and Atlanta, Grant chose Major General William Tecumseh Sherman. His choice was based on friendship, not on

Sherman's generalship. So far that had not been impressive. Early in the war, while commanding in Kentucky and Missouri, Sherman has so greatly exaggerated the strength of and danger from the enemy that he had suffered a nervous breakdown and had to be relieved. Returned to duty, he went to the opposite extreme by denying that the Confederates posed any threat at all, with the result that he was primarily to blame for the surprise and near destruction of Grant's army at Shiloh. In December 1862 his assault at Chickasaw Bluffs in Mississippi failed terribly, and during the subsequent Vicksburg campaign, although he ably did all that Grant told him to do, in truth he did not have to do very much. Assigned by Grant the starring role in the Battle of Chattanooga, his performance was so inept that only an impromptu attack by the troops of Major General George H. Thomas's Army of the Cumberland saved Grant from defeat and gave him victory.

Yet, despite this lackluster record, Grant deemed Sherman to be the best man to command in the West while he himself commanded in the East. He admired Sherman's brilliant intellect, boundless energy, and persistent enterprise. Above all he knew that Sherman was totally devoted to him personally and so could be trusted to make every effort to assist him in defeating the Confederacy in 1864.

On April 4, 1864, Grant sent Sherman his instructions. He was to "move against Johnston's army, to break it up, and get into the interior of the enemy's country as far as you can, inflicting all the damage you can against their war resources." The specific method by which Sherman accomplished this assignment, Grant added, he left to him, but he did ask Sherman to submit a broad "plan of operations." This Sherman did on April 10. After defining his mission as being to "knock Jos. Johnston, and to do as much damage to the resources of the enemy as possible," Sherman stated that he would compel Johnston to retreat to Atlanta, whereupon he would use his cavalry to cut the railroad between that city and Montgomery, Alabama, then "feign to the right, but pass to the left and act against Atlanta or its eastern communications, according to developed facts."

Superficially Sherman's plan seemed to comply with Grant's instructions. Actually it did not. Contrary to the clear implication of those instructions, Sherman proposed to make the capture of Atlanta and not the destruction of Johnston's army his prime objective. Several reasons, among them Sherman's personal distaste for battles with all of their uncertainties, explain this reversal of priorities, but the main one was that Sherman assumed that it would not be necessary for him to defeat Johnston because Grant soon would win the war by defeating Lee. Consequently, Sherman conceived his main task to be that of assuring Grant's success by preventing Johnston from

MAJOR GENERAL
WILLIAM T. SHERMAN

(LC)

sending reinforcements to Lee.

Grant took the same view of the matter. When he replied on April 19 to Sherman's April 10 letter he emphasized the need to forestall Johnston from aiding Lee. "If the enemy on your front," he cautioned Sherman, "shows signs of joining Lee, follow him up to the full extent of your ability."

To "knock Jos. Johnston" Sherman assembled at and near Chattanooga about 110,000 troops. By far the largest portion of them, nearly 65,000 infantry and artillerists, belonged to Major General George H. Thomas's Army of the Cumberland, which consisted of three corps: the IV, XIV, and XX, headed respectively by Major Generals Oliver Otis Howard, John M. Palmer, and "Fighting Joe" Hooker, who as commander of the

MAJOR GENERAL
GEORGE H. THOMAS

(BL)

Army of the Potomac in Virginia had come to grief against Lee at Chancellorsville in May of 1863. Thomas, because of his massive build, gave some the impression of being slow, and he was called the "Rock of Chickamauga" because of his stalwart defensive stand at that battle; yet his mind moved with lightning speed and at Nashville in December of 1864 he would deliver the most devastating attack of the entire war. On the basis of both record and talent he, not Sherman, deserved to command the campaign in Georgia, but he lacked what Sherman so amply possessed: the friendship and trust of Grant.

The next largest part of Sherman's host was Major General James B. McPherson's Army of the Tennessee (the Federals usually named their armies after rivers, hence the Army of the Tennessee, whereas Confederate practice was to name armies after states or portions thereof, thus the Army of Tennessee), about 23,000 soldiers organized into Major General John A. "Black Jack" Logan's XV Corps and the two-division XVI Corps and the two-division XVI Corps of Major General Grenville M. Dodge. It was Sherman's favorite army, for until recently he had commanded it, as had Grant before him. McPherson, its new commander, was intelligent and conscientious but, as events would reveal, deficient in initiative and enterprise.

Least among the major components of Sherman's invasion force was the so-called Army of the Ohio. Although Major General George Stoneman's cavalry division nominally formed part of it, for all practical purposes it consisted merely of the 11,000-man XXIII Corps, and its commander, Major General John M. Schofield, hitherto had seen little field service. But he was capable as well as ambitious, and during the campaign his small corps would accomplish much.

Sherman's artillery numbered 254 cannons, his cavalry about 11,000 troopers. The former was superior to its Confederate counterpart in all except the valor of its gun crews, having more rifled pieces and better ammunition. The latter, on the other hand, suffered from the poor leadership of its four division commanders, a situation made worse by the fact that the sole central control over its operations came from Sherman himself, and he lacked a realistic understanding of the limitations and potentialities of the mounted arm.

Sherman's chief concern was supplying his army as it marched and fought its way through northern Georgia. To do so he had to depend mainly on the Nashville and Chattanooga Railroad. When he assumed command in March it was delivering enough supplies to maintain the forces around Chattanooga but not enough to sustain an offensive. Therefore, he issued orders designed to remedy this situation. By the end of April an average of 135 freight cars a day were coming into Chattanooga—more than the minimum required. Sherman also collected 5,000 wagons and 32,000 mules to haul what the trains delivered, giving himself the means to operate away from the railroad

LIEUTENANT GENERAL WILLIAM J. HARDEE

(LC)

whenever that proved necessary or desirable.

To meet and, he hoped, defeat Sherman when he advanced, Johnston by the end of April had about 55,000 troops "present for duty," backed by 144 cannons. The infantry and most of the artillery were organized into two corps, those of Lieutenant Generals William J. Hardee and John Bell Hood, and the cavalry, which numbered approximately 8,500 and was commanded by Major General Joseph Wheeler.

Known as "Old Reliable," Hardee was a veteran of virtually all of the Army of Tennessee's battles. Following that army's humiliating rout at Chattanooga, he had become its acting commander, but when President Davis offered him the post on a regular basis he had declined it.

Hood, who was only thirty-two, had compiled a brilliant combat record as a brigade and division commander in Lee's Army of Northern Virginia, and at

Chickamauga his de facto corps's exploitation of a gap in the Union front produced the Confederate victory. His military success, however, had come at a high personal cost: at Gettysburg shrapnel paralyzed his left arm, at Chickamauga a bullet shattered his right thigh bone, necessitating amputation near the hip. As a result, he could not, despite an artificial leg, walk without the aid of crutches, and to ride he had to be strapped to his horse. Even so, his fighting spirit remained intact, and Johnston sought and welcomed his assignment to a corps command in the Army of Tennessee, calling it "my greatest comfort." He did not know that Hood had written Davis on April 13 deploring Johnston's failure to take the offensive: "When we are to be in a better condition to drive the enemy from our country I am not able to comprehend."

Wheeler had headed the Army of Tennessee's cavalry since the fall of 1862 and was energetic, aggressive, and resourceful. Unfortunately, he also (like most Civil War cavalry leaders) was unable to exercise effective control over units not under his personal supervision and had a penchant for exaggerating his

Known as "Old Reliable," Hardee was a veteran of virtually all of the Army of Tennessee's battles.

BEFORE THE MARCH ON ATLANTA, SHERMAN'S ARMIES GUARDED SUPPLY LINES AT PLACES LIKE WAUHATCHIE BRIDGE.

(USAMHI)

JOE BROWN'S PETS

Under the Confederate conscription laws, all able-bodied males between the ages of eighteen and forty-five were subject to military service except an assortment of exempted classes. Among those who were exempt were civil officials and officers in the state militia organizations. In Georgia, so many men of military age had gained exemption through state or county offices that they came to be called "Joe Brown's pets," after the controversial wartime governor. Howell Cobb, a political rival of Brown's, complained of districts that had gone without justices of the peace for years before the war that were served by several once hostilities began, and county courts suddenly saw flocks of clerks and deputy sheriffs although the war had virtually suspended all court business. These men were all fit for duty, Cobb said, as were the 2,726 militia officers who had only themselves to command, their enlisted members having all gone into the army.

Once Sherman invaded Georgia, Brown called out the civil servants and militia officers, directing their formation into companies and regiments. He ordered them to report to Atlanta, where they were organized into two brigades of three regiments apiece and a battalion of artillery: more than 3,000 men, altogether. Those

militia officers who were not elected for commissions in this new organization took up arms as enlisted men.

Major General Gustavus W. Smith took command of them in June, when they were assigned to guard the crossings of the Chattahoochee River. When Johnston anchored his army on Kennesaw Mountain, he ordered the militia north of the Chattahoochee to support the cavalry on his left. Under Smith the militia twice found itself within skirmishing distance of Federal forces, and it was among the last troops to fall back across the river. Johnston assigned the little division, which was now reduced to about 2,000 muskets, to the trenches east of Atlanta, along the Georgia Railroad.

In the Battle of Atlanta on July 22 the militia occupied works opposite the apex of the folded Union line and advanced against the XVII Corps when it retreated from Hardee's attack. The militia division was not heavily engaged, however, and only lost about fifty men in that engagement.

Early in August, as Sherman tightened the noose around Atlanta, Governor Brown called out the "reserve militia"--men between forty-six and fifty-five and boys aged sixteen or seventeen. Eventually some 2,000 such reserves reached General Smith, who noted that his division never exceeded 5,000 men. The militia suffered from a lack of both training and equipment. The first regiments of military and civil officers were armed from surplus army muskets, but most of the old

GENERAL GUSTAVUS SMITH

(USAMHI)

men and boys came with their own flintlocks, hunting rifles, and shotguns. More than two-thirds were never issued cartridge boxes, according to Smith.

In the final month of the siege the militia held the defenses west of the road to Marietta, and when the army retreated from Atlanta Smith's men acted as rear guard to Hood's reserve artillery train. The original regiments of civil and military officers had spent about a hundred days under arms by the time Atlanta fell, and for half that time they had been under fire. Smith and Hood both praised the militiamen for their performance during the campaign, but straggling on the retreat caused Smith to observe the imprudence of putting men over the age of fifty in the field. When the army had reassembled outside the city, Smith recommended a thirty-day furlough for his entire command, which was granted. In October the militia reassembled to contest Sherman's March to the Sea.

—William Marvel

successes and minimizing or concealing his failures. Nevertheless he gave Johnston's army what Sherman's lacked—a capable, experienced commander for its horsemen, who throughout the campaign would more than hold their own against the Union troopers.

The vast majority of the soldiers of both armies were battle-hardened veterans. This meant that they knew how to fight—and also when it was best not to fight. In particular, they took a dim view of charging a fortified enemy: "It don't pay." Owing to the almost total tactical dominance that the rifled musket gave the defense over the offense during the Civil War, rarely did frontal assaults succeed, and when they did the price usually was excessive, as witness Chickamauga, where the Confederates lost one-third of their total number in what proved to be a strategically barren victory. The reluctance of Billy Yank and Johnny Reb at this stage of the war to attack except when the foe was thought to be weak, or in the open, or to have an exposed flank would have a lot to do with what happened and did not happen once the campaign for Atlanta got under way.

FROM DALTON TO RESACA

A direct attack on Johnston at Dalton would require the Federals to penetrate Rocky Face Ridge, a chain of steep hills west of Dalton, by way of Buzzard Roost Gap. Not only was this a naturally strong position, but the Confederates had turned it, as Thomas put it, into a "slaughter pen" by means of fortifications,

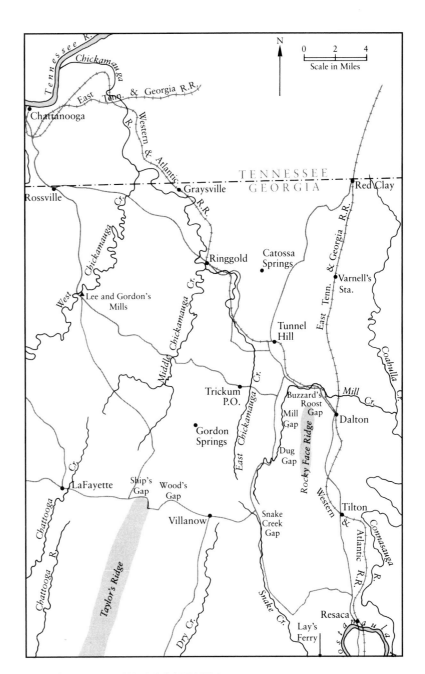

CHATTANOOGA TO OOSTANAULA
Thanks to Rocky Face Ridge, an almost continuous line of steep, rugged hills, Johnston's Confederate army enjoyed at Dalton a naturally strong defensive position which it had rendered virtually impregnable to frontal assault by fortifications and other obstacles at Buzzard Roost Gap, the main passageway through the ridge. Realizing this, Sherman feinted against Dalton with Thomas's Army of the Cumberland and Schofield's Army of the Ohio while sending McPherson's Army of the Tennessee swinging south via Snake Creek Gap to cut the Western & Atlantic Railroad, Johnston's supply line, at Resaca. This flanking move surprised Johnston and compelled him to evacuate Dalton, but owing to inadequate strength and his own lack of aggressiveness McPherson failed to cut the railroad and prevent Johnston from retreating unmolested to Resaca.

massed artillery, and damming a creek so as to create in front of it an artificial lake that could be crossed only by way of a railroad trestle. Therefore, Sherman early on decided not to try to break through this "terrible door of death." Instead he would force Johnston to abandon Dalton by outflanking him.

His initial plan for doing so called for McPherson's Army of the Tennessee to make a deep southward thrust to Rome, Georgia, thereby cutting Johnston's direct rail link to Alabama and threatening the Western & Atlantic Railroad, his supply line to Atlanta. The plan, however, was based on the assumption that before the campaign began, four, or at least two, additional divisions belonging to the Army of the Tennessee would reinforce McPherson. By May it was apparent that none of these divisions would arrive in time and that McPherson would continue to have just 23,000 troops, a force Sherman deemed too small to undertake safely so long a march so far from the rest of the Union army. Hence he needed a new plan and needed it quickly, for Grant had ordered the offensive in Georgia to begin at the same time as his in Virginia—May 5.

Such a plan was available. It came from Thomas. Back in February his cavalry had discovered an undefended mountain pass called Snake Creek Gap that led straight to Resaca, a railroad station on the north bank of the Oostanaula River eighteen miles south of Dalton. Why not, Thomas proposed to Sherman, send his Army of the Cumberland through Snake Creek Gap to Resaca where it would block both Johnston's line of supply and line of retreat?

Sherman adopted Thomas's plan—but with two major modifications. First, McPherson's Army of the Tennessee, not

the Army of the Cumberland, would execute the Snake Creek Gap maneuver. Second, instead of seizing and holding Resaca, McPherson was to break the railroad there, then fall back to Snake Creek Gap, where he would wait to pounce on Johnston's army as it retreated to Resaca as a consequence of having its supply line severed. Assailed on the flank by McPherson and from the rear by the pursuing Thomas and Schofield, the Confederates either would be destroyed or else forced to flee into the barren wilderness of northeast Georgia. Sherman believed that in this way he could achieve with less force and risk the same outcome Thomas's plan envisioned. It also would enable McPherson and the Army of the Tennessee to garner most of the glory of carrying out the move that produced the defeat of the Confederates in Georgia.

Johnston realized that the Federal offensive was about to start. Although he hoped that Sherman would oblige him with a frontal assault on Rocky Face Ridge, he expected him to do exactly what Sherman originally had intended to do—pretend to move against Dalton while sending a strong force to strike at Rome. Accordingly, on May 4 Johnston telegraphed Davis and Polk requesting that the latter send a division and a brigade from his Army of Mississippi to defend Rome. Davis promptly authorized Polk to go at once with a division and "any other available troops" to that town. Interpreting this statement literally, Polk headed for Georgia with practically all of his infantry—two divisions—and Major General William H. "Red" Jackson's cavalry division. Davis, on learning of what Polk had done, was dismayed—he wanted to retain all of Polk's cavalry in

Alabama-Mississippi so that it could raid Sherman's supply line—but decided to let Polk's move stand in the belief that Johnston now would have ample strength to repel Sherman and then at long last launch an offensive into Tennessee.

Starting on May 5, Thomas and Schofield advanced from the northwest and north toward Dalton while McPherson moved down from Chattanooga by way of Lee and Gordon's Mill, Ship Gap, and Villanow toward Snake Creek Gap. On May 8, having been notified that McPherson was a day's march from his

objective, Sherman ordered Thomas to engage the Confederates on Rocky Face and Schofield to feint an attempt to bypass it on the east. This they did, with some of Thomas's troops seizing the northern end of the ridge and others almost breaking through a weakly held pass called Dug Gap. Meanwhile, McPherson reached, then passed through, Snake Creek Gap. He met no opposition whatsoever and not so much as a single Confederate vedette patrolled the pass.

So oblivious was Johnston to the threat posed by Snake Creek Gap that on

HEADQUARTERS OF GENERAL THOMAS AT RINGGOLD, GEORGIA ON MAY 5.

(LC)

13

May 7 he had responded to a report that "McPherson's Corps" was moving southward from Lee and Gordon's Mill on the road to Lafayette by ordering Brigadier General George Cantey, commanding the garrison at Resaca, to come to Dalton. Fortunately, upon further consideration, he had canceled that order, but not until shortly after dark on May 8, when a telegram arrived from Cantey stating that "Cavalry scouts report Yankees in vicinity of Villanow today" did he become concerned about a possible enemy foray against Resaca via Snake Creek Gap. Even then, however, he thought that any attack on Resaca most likely would take the form of a cavalry raid and that Rome remained the true danger point. Therefore, he merely sent a Kentucky mounted brigade to reinforce Cantey, confident that it would give him sufficient strength to hold Resaca.

At mid-morning on May 9 McPherson set out from the southern end of Snake Creek Gap for Resaca, seven miles to the east. Although he had been instructed by Sherman to make a "bold and rapid movement," his march was cautious and slow, the consequence of "considerable resistance" from the Kentucky cavalry, dense undergrowth, and above all a growing fear on his part that a strong Confederate force might descend from the north and cut him off from the gap. Thus

THE BATTLE AT MILL CREEK GAP.

it was mid-afternoon before his advance reached and seized a hill overlooking Resaca.

Only about 4,000 Confederates, including the Kentuckians, defended the village and the railroad bridge over the nearby Oostanaula River, the destruction of which would cut Johnston's supply line. McPherson, in contrast, had at least 15,000 troops available for an attack, not counting a division he had detached to guard his rear. Nevertheless, he merely skirmished with the Confederates until evening, then withdrew to Snake Creek Gap. Subsequently he explained that Resaca appeared to be held by a "considerable force" which was "pretty well fortified" and that Dodge's XVI Corps was "all out of provisions." But his real reasons for not even attempting to take Resaca or at the very least tearing up some of the railroad track north of the place was that he believed he lacked sufficient strength to do these things and at the same time fend off an enemy thrust against his flank and rear from the direction of Dalton.

While understandable, McPherson's fear was unfounded. Not until the night of May 9 did Johnston learn, via cavalry reports, that "Logan and Dodge under McPherson are on an expedition to Resaca," whereupon he ordered two and a half divisions under Hood to Resaca. Thus McPherson had ample time and security in which to execute Sherman's instructions to break the railroad and then withdraw to Snake Creek Gap.

Having received a 2 P.M. message from McPherson that he was "within two miles of Resaca," Sherman lay down to sleep at midnight on May 9 confident that "I've got Joe Johnston dead!" Then, on the morning of May 10, another dispatch

arrived from McPherson in which he reported the failure to cut the railroad and the withdrawal to Snake Creek Gap. Disappointed and baffled—how could McPherson not have damaged the railroad at least a "little"?—Sherman decided to go ahead with a change in plan that Thomas and he had discussed yesterday, namely to march the entire army through Snake Creek Gap to Resaca in the hope of "interposing" it between Johnston and the Oostanaula.

On May 11 and 12 Hooker's XX Corps, followed by Palmer's XIV and Schofield's XXIII Corps, joined McPherson's forces at the mouth of Snake Creek Gap, leaving behind Howard's IV Corps to hold Johnston in check at

Dalton. Johnston, however, quickly detected what Sherman was doing and so on the night of May 12 retreated to Resaca. There, the following day, he deployed his army, which had been augmented by Major General William W. Loring's Division of what now in effect was Polk's Corps, along a line of hills to the west and north of Resaca, with its left anchored on the Oostanaula and its right flank covered by Wheeler's cavalry. (Official Confederate practice was to identify units above the level of regiment by the name

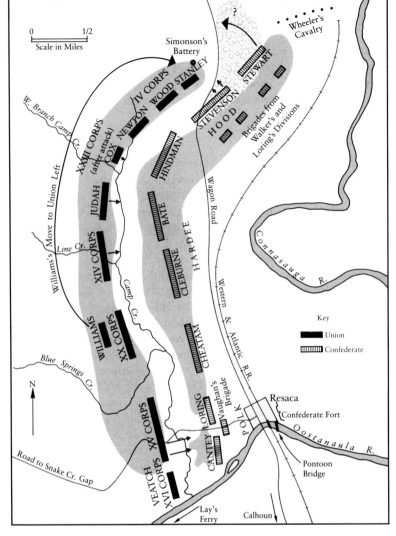

BATTLE OF RESACA, MAY 14

Assuming that Johnston was merely conducting a delaying action at Resaca to cover further retreat, Sherman ignored a proposal by Thomas to feint an attack against the Confederates there while sending a strong force across the Oostanaula to outflank them. Instead he launched an assault against the center of Johnston's line designed to pin down his army while Union cavalry cut the railroad south of Resaca. Johnston easily repulsed the assault, then had Stevenson's and Stewart's divisions of Hood's Corps strike the exposed Union left flank. Initially this thrust went well, but after being checked by Federal artillery it was driven back by a counterattack delivered by Williams's division of Hooker's XX Corps. Meanwhile, on the Union right, a portion of Logan's XV Corps stormed a hill overlooking Resaca and the bridges over the Oostanaula, then repelled Confederate efforts to retake it.

of their commanders whereas in the Union army all units had a numerical designation. This is why in the text corps is capitalized when referring to Polk's Corps and to the IV Corps, but not capitalized when a Union corps is described as being, for example, Howard's corps. The same holds true for references to divisions and brigades.) As he did so, Sherman advanced from Snake Creek Gap and took up a line roughly paralleling Johnston's. Meanwhile, the IV Corps occupied Dalton, then followed in the wake of the retreating Confederates and by evening was in supporting distance of the rest of the Union army.

During the Vicksburg campaign Sherman had become personally acquainted with Johnston's prudent tactics. Perhaps for this reason he assumed that Johnston would not attempt a serious stand at Resaca, with a river at his back, and instead merely would conduct a delaying action designed to cover a resumption of his retreat. Accordingly, on May 14 he ordered portions of the XX, XIV, and XXIII Corps to press the Confederate center in the belief that it would give way easily.

He could not have been more mistaken. Not only did the Confederates stop the Federal assaults cold, but Johnston launched a counterattack by the divisions of Major Generals Carter L. Stevenson and Alexander P. Stewart, both of Hood's Corps, with the object of turning the Union left, which was held by the IV Corps, and cutting Sherman off from Snake Creek Gap (what McPherson had feared would happen to him on May 9). Stevenson's Division overlapped, then struck the flank of Major General David S. Stanley's division of the IV Corps, driving it back in disarray. For a while only Captain Peter Simonson's six-gun battery, firing canister, kept the Rebels at bay. Then Brigadier General Alpheus S. Williams's division of the XX Corps, having been summoned from reserve in the center, came onto the field and with

deadly volleys drove back Stevenson's troops, thereby causing Stewart's to retreat also. Meanwhile, on the Union right, two brigades of the XV Corps stormed a hill overlooking Resaca and the railroad bridge, then beat off attempts to retake it in fierce fighting that continued until after dark.

Sherman now no longer believed that Johnston intended to retreat. Even so, his objective remained the same: push the Confederates to the bank of the Oostanaula, where he hoped to crush them as they tried to escape across that river. To that end, on the morning of May 15 the entire XX Corps shifted to the left of the IV Corps with orders to strike straight down the Dalton-Resaca wagon road. Then, early in the afternoon, two of its divisions, Major General Daniel Butterfield's and Brigadier General John Geary's, attacked the Confederate line at a point where it curved off to the

northeast. Despite a determined effort, they failed to reach, much less breach, the enemy defenses, which were manned by Major General Thomas C. Hindman's Division of Hood's Corps. They did, however, overrun a four-gun battery emplaced in front of the hill held by Hindman's troops—a success that Colonel Benjamin Harrison of the 70th Indiana claimed for his regiment and which would help him, twenty-four years later, to become president of the United States.

Encouraged by the repulse of the Union assault, Johnston decided to try

Hoping to drive Johnston's army back against the Oostanaula, Sherman ordered Howard's IV Corps and Hooker's XX Corps to attack the Confederate right wing from the north. The assault failed. After repulsing the Federals, Johnston directed Hood to have Stewart's Division make another attempt to turn Sherman's left. He learned that a strong enemy force had crossed the Oostanaula at Lay's Ferry. He sent a message calling off Stewart's attack, but before it could reach him Stewart advanced and suffered a bloody repulse from Williams's division of the XX Corps. During the night Johnston retreated across the Oostanaula, undetected by the Federals.

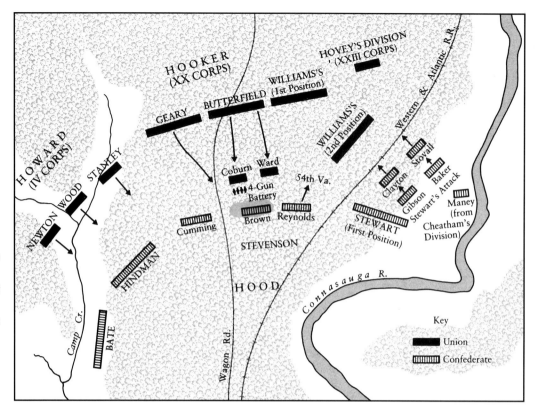

again what he attempted yesterday—turn Sherman's left and get into his rear. On his orders, transmitted through Hood, Stewart's Division swung around to the northwest before hitting what was thought to be a still vulnerable Federal flank. But as it did so, Johnston received word that the "Federal right" was crossing the Oostanaula several miles southwest of Resaca. At once Johnston directed Hood to call back Stewart. It was too late. Before Hood's message could reach him, Stewart attacked. Worse, he ran smack into Williams's XX Corps division, the one that blasted Stevenson's Division the day before. It now did the same to Stewart's troops, who lost heavily and gained nothing.

The Federal force reported to Johnston as having crossed the Oostanaula was Brigadier General Thomas Sweeny's division of the XVI Corps. Sweeny's assignment from Sherman was to put down pontoon bridges at Lay's

Ferry with a view to facilitating the pursuit of Johnston when he retreated from Resaca. In making it Sherman ignored a suggestion from Thomas on May 13 merely to feint an attack at Resaca while sending McPherson's army, bolstered by Hooker's XX Corps, across the Oostanaula to the hills west of Calhoun, a move that not only would have compelled Johnston to evacuate Resaca to preserve his supply line but also enabled McPherson to strike the Confederates with overwhelming force as they retreated southward.

Nonetheless, the Union bridgehead at Lay's Ferry rendered Resaca untenable and Johnston realized it. That night his troops stealthily withdrew from their fortifications and crossed the Oostanaula by means of a pontoon bridge and the railroad and wagon road bridges. Not until the Confederate rear guard set fire to the latter two structures shortly before dawn did the Federals discover that Johnston's army had escaped to fight another day.

Then and afterward Sherman blamed the failure to bag Johnston at Resaca on McPherson: he was "over-cautious" on May 9. No doubt that is true. Yet Sherman himself must bear a major share of the responsibility. Had he adopted Thomas's plan in its original form, or else supplemented the under-strength Army of the Tennessee with a corps from the Army of the Cumberland, he could have put a force through Snake Creek Gap capable of blocking Johnston's retreat and compelling him to fight a battle that almost surely would have led to the destruction of his army. Likewise, by not acting on Thomas's proposal to send McPherson and Hooker across the Oostanaula to the hills around Calhoun, Sherman threw away another opportunity to knock the Confederate army in Georgia out of the war, an achievement that would have freed his own army to join Grant in Virginia and crush Lee by sheer weight of numbers.

Johnston would forever claim that he was not caught off guard by Sherman's Snake Creek Gap maneuver and thus

never was in danger of being trapped and smashed north of the Oostanaula. The historical facts demonstrate otherwise. Only McPherson's loss of nerve and Sherman's mistakes saved Johnston from total and humiliating defeat at the very outset of the campaign for Atlanta.

FROM THE OOSTANAULA TO THE ETOWAH

Johnston's retreat took him to Calhoun, then on the following day (May 17) to Adairsville. At both places he planned to make a stand but on arriving at them found the terrain unfavorable. Then, as he examined his map, the idea for a brilliant stratagem came to him. This was to have Hardee's Corps and most of the cavalry continue due south by a road paralleling the Western & Atlantic to Kingston and for Hood's and Polk's Corps to march by a road leading southeast to Cassville. This might prompt the pursuing Sherman, calculated Johnston, to divide his army also, sending part of it toward Kingston and the rest toward Cassville. By doing so Sherman would expose himself

to a devastating counterblow, for on reaching Kingston Hardee would turn east and join Hood and Polk at Cassville, where their combined forces would attack and smash that part of the Union army heading for that town. At dawn on May 18 Hardee and Wheeler set out for Kingston while Hood and Polk marched toward Cassville.

Sherman reacted precisely as Johnston anticipated. Most of his army—the IV Corps, the XIV Corps (less a division which had gone to occupy Rome), and the Army of the Tennessee—followed Hardee, and the remainder, Hooker's and Schofield's corps, took the road to Cassville. Moreover, Sherman believed that Johnston's whole army was retreating to Kingston and therefore directed Hooker and Schofield to proceed to that town on reaching Cassville. Not even reports, conveyed to him by Hooker on the evening of May 18, that Confederate pickets had been encountered north of Cassville and that Rebel prisoners spoke of giving battle in that area, caused Sherman to modify his orders for all of the

GENERAL LEONIDAS POLK

(USAMHI)

army to concentrate at Kingston. As he saw it, the "broad, well-marked trail" left by Johnston's troops on the road to Kingston made it likely that any Confederates around Cassville were merely a detachment guarding a wagon train. In that case, then Stoneman's and Brigadier General Edward McCook's cavalry divisions, which had been sent yesterday to cut the railroad south of Cassville, would take care of them.

By the evening of May 18 Johnston's army, except for a small delaying force left at Kingston, was deployed in line of battle about one mile northwest of Cassville. Altogether it now numbered between 70,000 and 75,000 men thanks to the arrival of the rest of Polk's infantry, all of "Red" Jackson's cavalry, and other reinforcements. Yet when Hardee, Polk, and Hood urged advancing at once to strike the Federal column approaching Cassville, Johnston refused to do so; neither would he issue orders for tomorrow. Not until the morning of May 19 did he agree to a plan, presented by Hood, whereby Hood's Corps would form along a country road east of the Adairsville-Cassville road and attack the oncoming Federals in the flank while Polk assailed their front and Hardee covered Cassville on the west. Around

10:30 A.M. Hood began marching his corps up the country road. As he did so, a staff officer told him that there was a "dark line" off to the east. Hood looked and saw "a body of the enemy," apparently cavalry, approaching his rear along the road from Canton. At once he halted his march and sent a courier to notify Johnston of what was happening. "It can't be!" exclaimed Johnston on hearing the news, but after examining his map he muttered, "If that is so, General Hood will have to fall back at once." Soon afterward Johnston ordered his army to retire to a ridge about one-half mile southeast of Cassville.

The Union cavalry that appeared so unexpectedly in Hood's rear consisted of McCook's division followed by Stoneman's. They were attempting to carry out Sherman's order to raid the Western & Atlantic Railroad south of Cassville and did not anticipate finding a large Confederate force in the vicinity. Indeed, neither then nor later did they realize that they had prevented a potentially devastating attack on Hooker's corps by Hood and Polk, thereby performing the greatest service rendered by Sherman's cavalry during the whole Atlanta campaign!

On reaching the ridge southeast of Cassville, Hood's Corps took position on

Yet when Hardee, Polk, and Hood urged advancing at once to strike the Federal column approaching Cassville, Johnston refused to do so.

the right and Polk's on the left, while Hardee's formed to the south of it, guarding the road to Cass Station. During the afternoon the IV Corps, marching from Kingston, where Sherman finally had discovered that he had been following a false trail, deployed along a parallel ridge where it soon was joined on the left by the XX Corps and Brigadier General Jacob D. Cox's division of the XXIII Corps and on the right by two divisions of the XIV Corps. Neither Johnston nor Sherman proposed to attack, the former because he hoped the Federals would assault him, the latter because he assumed that most of the Confederate army already was south of the Etowah River and that the force facing him at Cassville was only a rear guard that would retreat as soon as it was dark.

Again Sherman assumed wrongly. Not only did he have Johnston's entire army before him, but Johnston had no intention of retreating. He considered his new position superb—"the best that I ever saw occupied during the war," he later would assert—and he rejected a warning from his chief of artillery, Brigadier General Francis Shoup, that part of the ridge was vulnerable to enemy cannon

fire. Besides, that morning he had issued a proclamation telling his soldiers that their retreating had ended and that they now would give battle to the invaders. Not to make good on these words was an embarrassment he wished to avoid.

Late in the afternoon the Federal batteries opened up and soon demonstrated that Shoup's warning was justified as they ravaged Polk's and Hood's troops with cross and enfilade fire until nightfall ended the bombardment. Alarmed, Polk and Hood requested Johnston to meet them at Polk's headquarters. When Johnston arrived, Polk told him that his corps would be unable to hold its position more than an hour when the Yankee cannonade resumed in the morning and Hood stated that he would have to abandon his line in two hours. For a while Johnston tried to persuade the two generals that they exaggerated the danger, but when Hood insisted that the only alternative to a retreat was an attack, he ordered the former. Starting at midnight the Confederates pulled out of their works and headed for the Etowah. On the afternoon of May 20 they crossed that river, then burned the railroad and wagon road

ALLATOONA AS SEEN
FROM THE BANKS OF
THE ETOWAH.

(LC)

bridges spanning it. Sherman, still thinking that the enemy had only a rear guard at Cassville, did not pursue.

So ended the second week and the second phase of the campaign. Manifestly its course favored Sherman. At the moderate cost of probably no more than 5,000 casualties he had forced Johnston to retreat one-half of the hundred miles from Dalton to Atlanta. In Richmond, Jefferson Davis began to grow uneasy. So did many other Southerners, particularly those in Georgia, and above all those in Atlanta. When and where would Johnston stand and fight Sherman? Would he stand and fight him at all?

THE "HELL HOLE" (MAY 21–JUNE 6)

Once across the Etowah, Johnston halted at Allatoona, a position naturally stronger than the one he occupied at Dalton. Aware of this, Sherman again resorted to a flanking move, one that took him away from his railroad lifeline. On May 23 his troops, who had been instructed to carry ten days' rations, crossed the Etowah near Kingston and advanced to the west of Allatoona in three columns, with the XV and XVI Corps on the right, the IV and XIV Corps in the center, and Hooker and Schofield as before on the left. Sherman believed that this maneuver not only would cause Johnston to evacuate Allatoona but also result in his falling back to or even beyond the Chattahoochee River, only a few miles from Atlanta. "We are all in motion," Sherman confidently telegraphed the head of his quartermaster bureau in Nashville, "like a vast hive of bees, and

A WARTIME PHOTOGRAPH OF ALLATOONA PASS.

(USAMHI)

expect to swarm along the Chattahoochee in five days."

Again Sherman indulged in wishful thinking. Johnston anticipated Sherman's move, and when his cavalry confirmed it he sent his army marching toward Dallas, a crossroads village which he correctly judged was Sherman's immediate objective. By the morning of May 25 all of his forces were deployed in the Dallas area, with Hardee's Corps on the left, Polk's in the center, and Hood's on the right where it covered a road that passed by a Methodist chapel called New Hope Church.

This road was not on the Union maps. Consequently, on reaching it Geary's division of Hooker's corps took it in the belief that it led to Dallas. Instead, of course, it led to Hood's Corps. At once Thomas and Hooker ordered Geary, whom they accompanied, to halt and dig in. At the same time they summoned Williams's and Butterfield's divisions to hasten to Geary's aid and notified Sherman that the enemy was in their front and in great strength. Sherman, however, scoffed at their report, for he assumed that if Johnston made a stand at all north of the Chattahoochee, it would be at Marietta.

sen to fight at Dallas rather than at Marietta, Sherman spent May 26 deploying his forces for another attack. This took the form on May 27 of sending Howard with two divisions (Brigadier General Thomas J. Wood's of the IV Corps and Brigadier General Richard W. Johnson's of the XIV Corps) to turn the Confederate right flank. That afternoon at Pickett's Mill on Little Pumpkinvine Creek, Howard found what he thought was the end of the enemy line and so ordered Brigadier General William B. Hazen's brigade of Wood's division to attack it. Unfortunately for Hazen's troops and those of another of Wood's brigades, Colonel William H. Gibson's, who followed them into action, the Confederates had detected Howard's movement and perceived its purpose. As a result, Hazen's and Gibson's men encountered, not an open flank, but Major General Patrick Cleburne's elite division of Hardee's Corps, which hurled them back with over one thousand casualties, nearly half of them killed, while suffering a comparatively light loss itself. Ironically, just as Howard began his assault, Sherman concluded that "it is useless to look for the flank of the enemy, as he makes tempo-

Therefore, when Williams and Butterfield reinforced Geary, Sherman ordered Hooker to attack the Confederates at New Hope Church, confident that they were few in number and that Hooker would break through easily and thus open the way to Marietta. Spearheaded by Williams's division, the XX Corps delivered a series of assaults that continued until dark. Stewart's Division alone sufficed to beat back all of them, inflicting nearly 700 casualties and gaining a measure of revenge for its bloody repulse ten days ago at Resaca.

Still skeptical that Johnston had cho-

THE TWO ARMIES WERE VIRTUALLY ON TOP OF EACH OTHER DURING THE MAY 25 BATTLE AT NEW HOPE CHURCH AS ILLUSTRATED BY A. R. WAUD.

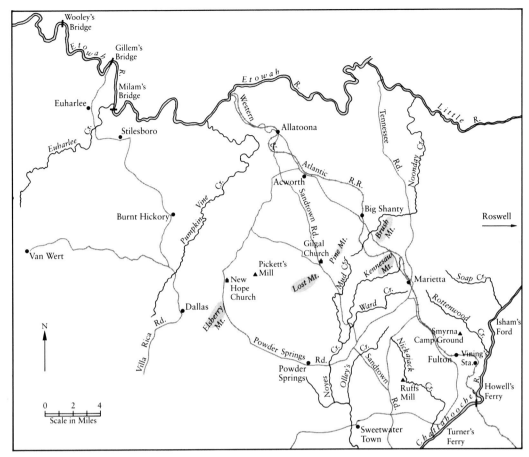

ETOWAH TO
CHATTAHOOCHEE
*Johnston retreated
across the Etowah to
Allatoona, a defen-
sive position natural-
ly stronger than
Dalton. Sherman
again resorted to a
flanking move,
swinging his whole
army to the east of
Allatoona. He
believed that this
would cause
Johnston to with-
draw to the
Chattahoochee.
Instead Johnston
blocked Sherman's
advance on May 25
at New Hope Church,
where Hood's Corps
repelled an assault
by Hooker's XX
Corps. Sherman
attempted to turn the
Confederate right
flank but suffered a
bloody repulse at
Pickett's Mill on May
27. In turn Bate's
Division of Hardee's
Corps made a poorly
executed attack on
Sherman's right at
Dallas on May 28.
Unable to advance,
Sherman abandoned
his attempt to reach
the Chattahoochee
by this route and fell
back to Acworth
early in June.
Johnston thereupon
established a new
defense line north of
Kennesaw Mountain.*

rary breastworks as fast as we travel" and so sent a message to Howard to halt and go on the defensive!

This Howard did and it was well that he did. Receiving word from Wheeler that Howard's left on Little Pumpkinvine Creek was "in the air," Hood asked and received Johnston's permission to strike that flank. However, after his corps spent the night marching to that point, Hood learned that Howard's force now was on the west side of the creek behind a line of breastworks facing east. Hood forth-with notified Johnston that the enemy flank no longer was vulnerable, where-upon Johnston directed him to return to his position on the Confederate front.

Next Johnston, having received reports that McPherson's troops were withdrawing from the line they had estab-lished east of Dallas, instructed Hardee to have Major General William Bate ascertain

whether this was true, and if so to attack. Bate in turn ordered Brigadier General Frank Armstrong's Brigade of Jackson's cavalry to charge the Federal works at Dallas; should it encounter little or no resistance, then four cannon shots would be fired as a signal for Bate's Division, which was on Armstrong's right, to attack. At about 3:45 P.M. Armstrong's troopers, dismounted, rushed forward, only to be driven back by withering fire from the XV Corps. Obviously McPherson had not withdrawn, hence Bate's signal cannons remained silent. Even so, two of Bate's brigades, Findley's Floridians and Lewis's Kentuckians (the famed "Orphan Brigade"), thinking that a full-fledged bat-tle was under way and that they had not heard the cannons, advanced through the dense woods and underbrush in the expectation of hitting a retreating enemy in the open. Instead they were hit with a

Sherman now had to accept the fact that the entire Confederate army stood in his way and was determined to stay there.

storm of bullets, shells, and canister which cost them over 1,000 casualties before they could be recalled. It was a fiasco that balanced out the Federal one at Pickett's Mill.

Sherman now had to accept the fact that the entire Confederate army stood in his way and was determined to stay there. Worse, his own army, because it experienced difficulty supplying itself so far from the railroad, began to run short of food and forage. Consequently, he ordered a withdrawal from around Dallas and Pickett's Mill, an area his troops had dubbed the "Hell Hole." This proved to be a hard, slow process, made all the more so by false alarms of another Confederate assault on McPherson. Not until June 6 did the Union forces reach the Western & Atlantic at Acworth and thus reestablish their supply line.

On the whole Johnston performed well during this phase of the campaign. He anticipated and blocked Sherman's thrust toward the Chattahoochee, kept him pinned down for nearly two weeks while inflicting heavy casualties, and finally forced him to pull back. Sherman, on the other hand, once more displayed a penchant for basing his plans on wishful

MAJOR GENERAL JOHN LOGAN RALLIES HIS TROOPS AT DALLAS ON MAY 28.

(FRANK AND MARIE WOOD PRINT COLLECTION)

thinking and an obstinate unwillingness to change them when it should have been apparent to him that they were unrealistic. Yet he also again compelled Johnston to relinquish a strong position (Allatoona), and despite the withdrawal to Acworth his army advanced still closer to Atlanta, where the sound of the fighting at New Hope Church, Pickett's Mill, and Dallas could be heard. To the people there it was an ominous sound, and some of them left the city or made preparations to do so should the Yankees draw much nearer.

KENNESAW MOUNTAIN (JUNE 7–JULY 2)

Sherman spent four days at Acworth waiting for the railroad bridge over the Etowah to be rebuilt. On June 10, that task having been accomplished, he began advancing along the line of the Western & Atlantic. With him, just arrived, was the XVII Corps of the Army of the Tennessee. Commanded by Major General Francis P. Blair, Jr., its two divisions of 9,000 veterans more than made good Sherman's battle losses of the past month.

Late on the morning of June 10 the Union vanguard reached Big Shanty (present-day Kennesaw) and found itself confronted by a ten-mile-long Confederate defense line that stretched from Brush Mountain on the east through Pine Mountain in the center to Gilgal Church on the west. Sherman, who had promised Major General Henry W. Halleck, the Union army's chief of staff in Washington, that "I will not run head on [against] his [the enemy's] fortifications," deployed his forces parallel to this line and instructed

Thomas to have the IV and XIV Corps work their way around Pine Mountain, a move he believed would compel Johnston to retreat because that elevation constituted a vulnerable salient in the Confederate front.

By June 14, despite incessant rains that turned the fields and roads into quagmires, the IV Corps was close to achieving this objective. While observing its operations Sherman noticed some Confederates atop Pine Mountain (actually a hill only about 300 feet high) who were making no attempt to conceal themselves. "How saucy they are!" he exclaimed, then told Howard to have a battery fire at them. Howard passed on the order to Captain Peter Simonson, whose cannons had checked Stevenson's Division during the first day of fighting at Resaca exactly one month before.

Unknown and unknowable to Sherman, among the "saucy" Confederates were Johnston, Hardee, and Polk, discussing whether or not to evacuate Pine Mountain. The first shot from Simonson's battery caused them to scatter, the second (probably) struck Polk in the left side and ripped through his chest, eviscerating him. (Three days later a Confederate sniper killed Simonson). The Episcopal bishop of Louisiana as well as a general—he often was referred to as the "Bishop General"—Polk had in the pockets of his uniform coat *The Book of Common Prayer* and four copies of a newly published tract entitled *Balm for the Weary and Wounded*, three copies of which were inscribed to Johnston, Hardee, and Hood. Major General William Loring assumed acting command of Polk's Corps.

During the night the Confederates withdrew from Pine Mountain. On learning of this in the morning, Sherman

jumped to the conclusion that Johnston was retreating all along his front and so ordered his forces to pursue, hoping to catch the enemy in the open. Once more he was overoptimistic. Johnston did fall back, but from one strong position to another, until on June 19 he reached the strongest one of all: Kennesaw Mountain. This was (is) a long ridge (two miles) slanting to the southwest and consisting of three knobs: Big Kennesaw at the northeast end, Little Kennesaw in the middle, and a spur today called Pigeon Hill at the lower end. Loring's troops occupied Big and Little Kennesaw, Hardee's covered the southern extension, and Hood's Corps and Wheeler's cavalry guarded the area to the east of the mountain and nearby Marietta.

Sherman reacted to Johnston's new defense line by deploying the Army of the Tennessee opposite Hood and the Army of the Cumberland facing Loring and Hardee. At the same time he sent Schofield with his XXIII Corps down the Sandtown road with instructions to try to find a point where Johnston's left flank could be turned. This move caused Johnston, on the night of June 21, to counter it by switching Hood's Corps from the right to the left and extending Loring's front eastward so as to cover the area vacated by Hood.

During the morning of June 22

Hooker's corps, on orders from Sherman relayed by Thomas, shifted southward to Kolb's Farm on the Powder Springs road, where it linked up with Schofield's forces on its right. Hood, evidently unaware of Schofield's presence, thought he saw an opportunity to overpower Hooker and then roll up the entire Union right flank. Hence, without notifying Johnston, he attacked with Stevenson's and Hindman's Divisions along and to the north of the Powder Springs road.

Fiasco, not victory, awarded Hood's impulsive initiative. Stevenson's troops encountered such heavy fire from Williams's division and a brigade of Cox's division that they either broke or went to ground, and Geary's cannons alone sufficed to stop, then turn back, Hindman's assault. Altogether the Confederates suffered about 1,500 casualties whereas the Federals lost no more than 250 men. Understandably, Hood did not so much as mention the Battle (if such it can be

called) of Kolb's Farm in his memoirs.

But if Hood failed in his attempt to smash Sherman's right, the presence of his corps south of Kennesaw frustrated Sherman's attempt to get around Johnston's left. And Sherman already was feeling very frustrated. A month now had passed since he crossed the Etowah expecting to reach and perhaps pass over the Chattahoochee in a few days. Yet he still had not achieved that goal and there seemed to be no immediate prospect that he would. Instead he was becoming, so he feared, bogged down in a stalemate—a stalemate that might enable Johnston to do the one thing above all he must not be allowed to do, transfer troops to Virginia to aid Lee against Grant.

So it was that Sherman, declaring that "flanking is played out," on June 25 ordered Thomas and McPherson to "break through" Johnston's line with frontal assaults. Although both generals doubted that the attacks could succeed, both dutifully proceeded to carry them out. On the morning of June 27, following a furious but ineffective artillery bombardment, Brigadier General Morgan L. Smith's division of the XV Corps, which by now had been shifted to the west of Kennesaw, assailed the Confederate positions around Pigeon Hill while further to the south Brigadier General John C. Newton's division of the IV Corps and Brigadier General Jefferson C. Davis's division of the XIV Corps did the same against what had become Johnston's center (see map). Smith's and Newton's troops, despite a determined effort, failed even to reach the Rebel works, and although a few of Davis's men, thanks to favorable terrain, managed to scale the enemy ramparts on what henceforth would be known as

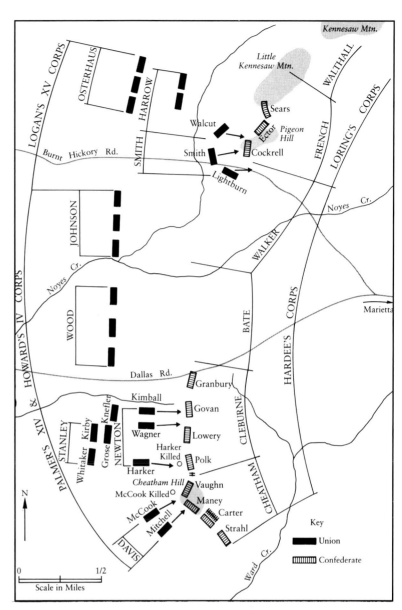

BATTLE OF KENNESAW MOUNTAIN, JUNE 27

On June 10 Sherman, his army having been reinforced by Blair's XVII Corps, launched a new offensive designed to drive Johnston back to and across the Chattahoochee. The Confederates fell back slowly until they reached Kennesaw Mountain, an immensely strong position that they made stronger still with fortifications. Here they not only halted Sherman's advance but frustrated his efforts to outflank them. Fearing a stalemate that might enable Johnston to reinforce Lee against Grant in Virginia, Sherman decided to try to break through the enemy defenses with a frontal attack. On the morning of June 27 a division of the XV Corps assailed Johnston's right at Pigeon Hill and a division each from the IV and XIV Corps did the same against his center. Both assaults failed with heavy losses. Meanwhile, however, Cox's division of Schofield's XXIII Corps worked its way to a point south of Kennesaw where it would be possible to turn the Confederate left flank. On learning this, Sherman transferred McPherson's Army of the Tennessee from his left to the right, thereby compelling Johnston to retreat on the night of July 2.

Cheatham's Hill (named after the commander of the Confederate troops who held the hill, Major General Benjamin F. Cheatham), they either were killed or captured and their surviving comrades forced to take cover just below the crest of the hill. It was all over in less than an hour, during which the Federals suffered nearly 3,000 casualties whereas the Confederate loss came to no more than 700 men, most of them pickets overrun in the initial Union rush. Such were the results of Sherman doing what he had told Halleck he would not do—"run head on" against fortifications.

Sherman's first reaction to the repulse, which he attributed to his troops attacking with insufficient "vigor," was to ask Thomas, "Can you break any part of the enemy line today?" Politely but firmly Thomas answered in the negative. The only way, he added, that the Confederate works could be taken would be by a regular siege-style operation. Sherman, as Thomas doubtlessly expected, rejected this approach for it would prolong the stalemate indefinitely.

Thus Sherman found himself left with only one alternative—another flanking maneuver. But where? The answer came late that afternoon in a message from Schofield: Cox's division, working its way southward, had reached a point where it appeared that the Confederate line terminated. After requesting and receiving confirmation of this intelligence from Schofield, Sherman asked Thomas if he was willing to risk a large-scale attempt to turn Johnston's left. Thomas's reply was both prompt and blunt: "I think it decidedly better than butting against breastworks twelve feet thick and strongly abatized." ("Abatized" referred to abatis— sharpened stakes affixed in a crisscross fashion to logs which served the same defensive function as modern-day barbed wire.)

Because Schofield's corps was too small and Thomas's forces already stretched to their safe limit, Sherman also had no choice except to employ McPherson's three corps for the turning movement, even though that would mean abandoning a direct connection with the railroad. (Ironically, when Thomas on June 23 proposed taking advantage of Hood's shift to the Confederates' left by having McPherson swing around their

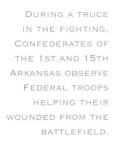

At long last the way was open for Sherman's men to "swarm" along the Chattahoochee.

DURING A TRUCE IN THE FIGHTING, CONFEDERATES OF THE 1ST AND 15TH ARKANSAS OBSERVE FEDERAL TROOPS HELPING THEIR WOUNDED FROM THE BATTLEFIELD.

(FROM *MOUNTAIN CAMPAIGNS IN GEORGIA*)

right, Sherman refused on the grounds that it would expose the railroad and his forward supply bases to enemy seizure. Had such a move been made, almost surely it would have led to Johnston's immediate retreat, as only a thin screen of infantry and Wheeler's cavalry guarded Kennesaw and Marietta from a Union thrust from the east).

Early on the morning of July 2 Morgan Smith's division of the XV Corps left its trenches west of Pigeon Hill and headed down the Sandtown road, to be followed during the night by the rest of the XV Corps and the XVI and XVII Corps. That same night Johnston, who long had anticipated precisely this movement and saw no way of countering it, evacuated his lines on and around Kennesaw and retreated southward through Marietta. At long last the way was open for Sherman's men to "swarm" along the Chattahoochee.

ACROSS THE CHATTAHOOCHEE (JULY 3–17)

Assuming that Johnston would retreat beyond the Chattahoochee and hoping to catch him before he did, Sherman ordered a vigorous pursuit. As usual when it came to assessing Johnston's intentions, he was wrong. Two weeks before Johnston, at the urging of his chief of artillery, Brigadier General Shoup, had authorized the construction of a fortified line along the north bank of the Chattahoochee where it would cover the railroad bridge. After a halt at Smyrna Camp Ground on July 3–4, he withdrew to this position on July 5. Although

THE SOUTH BANK OF THE CHATTAHOOCHEE RIVER WITH CONFEDERATE WORKS IN THE FOREGROUND.

(LC)

Johnston had done the same at Resaca, Sherman at first refused to believe that "such a general as he" would fight with a river to his back. Not until Sherman made a personal reconnaissance did he admit that indeed this was the case. He also concluded that the new enemy line could not be carried by assault and so, like all of the previous ones, it would have to be outflanked.

There were two ways that could be done. One was to cross the Chattahoochee downstream from the fortifications (to the southwest), the other was to cross upstream from there (to the northeast). Johnston expected Sherman to adopt the first approach: not only would this place him closer to Atlanta but hitherto all of his large-scale flanking maneuvers had been to his right. Instead, Sherman chose the second option, for unlike the first it would enable him to keep his army between the Confederates and the vital railroad.

Accordingly, on July 8 Schofield, acting on Sherman's instructions, secured a bridgehead on the south (actually west) side of the Chattahoochee at Isham's Ford, and on the following day Brigadier General Kenner Garrard's cavalry division did the same further north at Roswell.

31

Neither Schofield nor Garrard encountered serious resistance because none was present owing to Johnston's assumption that Sherman would attempt to cross downstream. On the night of July 9 Johnston, realizing that he had been outgeneraled and that his position now was untenable, withdrew his army to the other side of the river, burned the railroad bridge, and then established his headquarters at the Dexter Niles house, a mere three miles from the center of Atlanta. In the city, when they learned of the retreat, hundreds of the inhabitants fled, and the evacuation of military hospitals and machinery, already under way, accelerated.

Sherman refrained from an immediate pursuit. His troops needed to rest and catch their psychological breath before making a final lunge at Atlanta. Besides,

he no longer felt compelled to maintain constant pressure on Johnston. On June 28, just one day after his bloody, futile assault at Kennesaw, he had received a telegram from Halleck in Washington. It read:

Lieutenant General Grant directs me to say that the movements of your army may be made entirely independent of any desire to retain Johnston's forces where they are. He does not think Lee will bring any additional troops to Richmond, on account of the difficulty of feeding them.

Behind these words lay the story of the campaign in Virginia. There Grant had engaged Lee in a series of titanic battles, seeking to deliver a knockout blow. Each time Lee had held his own, inflicting ghastly casualties on the Federals, who usually did the attacking. Only by means of flanking moves had Grant been able to force Lee back to the defenses of Richmond. But there he had been stopped. Worse, in the fighting his army lost over 60,000 men and with them its offensive capability: the survivors simply

GENERAL HENRY HALLECK

(LC)

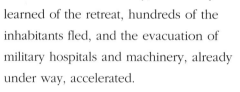

MAJOR GENERAL GRENVILLE DODGE'S XVI CORPS CROSSES THE CHATTAHOOCHEE AT ROSWELL'S FERRY.

(FRANK AND MARIE WOOD PRINT COLLECTION)

were unwilling to charge the Confederate trenches, fearful of another slaughter such as the one on June 3 at Cold Harbor where 7,000 Federals were mowed down in less than ten minutes in a vain effort to pierce Lee's thin line. Grant realized this, and though he would keep trying, he also realized that it was unlikely that he would defeat Lee or take Richmond in the near future.

That is why he had Halleck send the message to Sherman that he did. In effect, he told Sherman that it was up to him to achieve in Georgia what he, Grant, had failed to accomplish in Virginia—a war-winning victory or a victory that would cause the Northern people to believe that the war was being won. This meant that Sherman, not Grant, henceforth had the star role in the strategic drama of 1864.

Even as Sherman moved to the center of the military stage, Johnston was about to be removed from it. Jefferson Davis was dismayed by Johnston's failure to try to defeat Sherman in an all-out battle, alarmed by his incessant retreats, and unconvinced by that general's explanation for both, namely that he was too heavily outnumbered either to attack Sherman successfully or to block his flanking moves. Moreover, to urgings from Davis's chief of staff, General Braxton Bragg, that Wheeler's cavalry be used to cut Sherman's supply line, Johnston answered that he needed it to protect his flanks and that therefore cavalry from elsewhere—in particular Nathan Bedford Forrest's in Mississippi—should be sent to perform this mission. Were that done, Johnston contended, Sherman would be compelled to retreat and the Army of Tennessee could go over to the offensive.

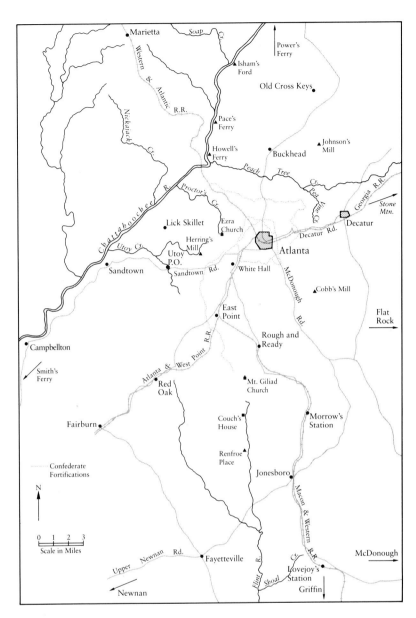

ATLANTA AREA

From Kennesaw Johnston withdrew to a fortified line covering the railroad on the northwest bank of the Chattahoochee. Knowing that a direct attack on this position merely would repeat the Kennesaw slaughter, Sherman outflanked it by sending detachments across the Chattahoochee at Isham's Ford and Roswell. Johnston, who had expected Sherman to attempt to turn his left rather than right flank, thereupon retreated on the night of July 9 to the other side of the Chattahoochee and within a few miles of Atlanta. Sherman, wishing to rest and resupply his troops before entering into what he believed would be the final phase of the campaign, made no attempt to follow with his full force until July 17. On that very same day Confederate President Jefferson Davis, having decided that Johnston could not be trusted to make a determined effort to hold Atlanta, replaced him as commander with Hood.

Whether he realized it or not, Johnston in effect was saying that he could not stop Sherman through his own efforts. To Davis, this was intolerable. For if Sherman was not stopped—that is, if Atlanta was not held—then all that had been achieved by Lee stopping Grant and holding Richmond would be wasted and the Confederate strategy of winning by not losing foiled.

There were three things Davis could have done. The first was to send Forrest, as Johnston insisted, against Sherman's supply line. The problem with that was that Forrest was needed to defend Mississippi against Union incursions that Sherman had ordered for the precise pur-

politically it would be a risky step. Besides, with whom could he replace him? Hence he perforce followed the third course open to him, namely to hope that Johnston ultimately would fight and defeat Sherman, or at the very least prevent him from taking Atlanta.

This hope all but disappeared when Johnston retreated across the Chattahoochee to the very outskirts of Atlanta. As soon as he learned of it Davis sent Braxton Bragg to Atlanta to ascertain what plans, if any, Johnston had for defending the city and whether it would be best to replace him with Hardee or Hood. Bragg arrived in Atlanta by train on July 13 and spent two days conferring

PONTOON BOATS WERE USED TO FERRY TROOPS AND EQUIPMENT ACROSS THE MANY RIVERS AND CREEKS.

(LC)

pose of keeping him pinned there. For him to go into Tennessee or Georgia would be to abandon both Mississippi and Alabama, and that in turn would deprive the Army of Tennessee of its main source of supplies. Forrest, therefore, had to stay where he was.

Davis's second option was to remove Johnston from command. He very much wanted to do so. But militarily and

with Johnston and his generals, especially Hood, from whom he obtained a memorandum criticizing Johnston's conduct of the campaign and claiming that he was the sole top commander in the Army of Tennessee to have favored an offensive policy. On July 15 Bragg telegraphed Davis that he could not learn that Johnston "has any more plan for the future than he has had in the past," and

that to replace him with Hardee "would perpetuate the past and present policy of retreat" that Hardee "has advised and now sustains."

Bragg's statement about Johnston was true. His assertion concerning Hardee was a lie motivated by a personal grudge against him going back to the time when Bragg commanded the Army of Tennessee. Perhaps Davis, on reading it, suspected that it was false, for he had a letter from Hardee complaining about Johnston's passivity. In any event he decided to give Johnston one last chance. On the morning of July 16 he telegraphed him: "I wish to hear from you as to present situation, and your plan of operations so specifically as to enable me to anticipate events." That evening Johnston answered:

As the enemy has double our number, we must be on the defense. My plan of operations must, therefore, depend on that of the enemy. It is mainly to watch for an opportunity to fight to advantage. We are trying to put Atlanta in condition to be held for a day or two by the Georgia militia, that army movements may be freer and wider.

When, on the morning of July 17, Davis read these words he hesitated no longer. Johnston, it was obvious, could not be depended on to make a determined, all-out effort to hold Atlanta. As for Hardee, even if what Bragg had said about him was untrue, the fact remained that back in December he had declined the permanent command of the Army of Tennessee, an indication of a fear of responsibility that could be fatal given the present circumstances of that army. Thus Johnston's replacement had to be Hood: only he could be trusted

to fight, and to fight hard, for Atlanta. That afternoon the Confederate War Department transmitted telegrams to Johnston and Hood notifying the former that he was relieved of command and the latter that he now commanded, with the temporary rank of full general, the Army of Tennessee.

As these telegrams made their way from Richmond to Atlanta, Sherman's army crossed the Chattahoochee, with McPherson and Schofield heading for Decatur, east of Atlanta, and Thomas moving directly on the city from the north. Sherman thought it probable that Johnston would give battle, but he also deemed it possible he would again retreat. Either way, Sherman was confident that soon Atlanta would be his.

HOOD FIGHTS FOR ATLANTA

Johnston and Hood received their respective telegrams on the night of July 17. Early in the morning Hood went to Johnston's headquarters. There he joined

LIEUTENANT GENERAL
JOHN B. HOOD

(USAMHI)

with Hardee and Stewart, who now with the rank of lieutenant general headed Polk's Corps, in sending a telegram to Davis asking him to retain Johnston in command until a battle deciding the fate of Atlanta was fought. Davis refused. To suspend the order relieving Johnston, he telegraphed back, would make "the case worse than it was before the order was issued." Hood thereupon formally assumed command and Johnston went to Atlanta from whence, the following day, he and his wife took a train to Macon. In all likelihood he was relieved at being relieved: should Atlanta fall, not he but Hood would be blamed and his cherished military reputation would be preserved.

In his July 15 report to Davis, Bragg had also asserted that naming Hood to command would give "unlimited satisfaction." This too was a lie. Reaction in the Army of Tennessee to Johnston being superseded by Hood was generally, although not universally, negative. Like his good friend George B. McClellan, Johnston had a knack for making himself popular with the rank and file. On the other hand, Hood's well-known penchant for the offensive filled many veterans with apprehension. Last, but not least, Hardee bitterly resented not obtaining the command himself and having to serve under a man who was his junior in rank as well as years.

BATTLE OF PEACHTREE CREEK

In becoming commander, Hood took on the task of stopping, or better still defeating, Sherman. How was he to do it? On July 19 his cavalry reported that

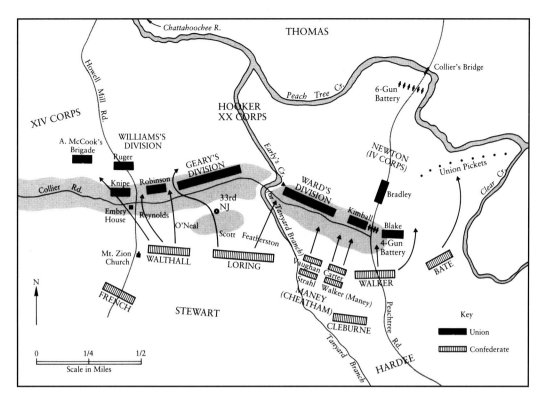

Map labels:
Chattahoochee R. · THOMAS · Collier's Bridge · Howell Mill Rd. · Peach Tree Cr. · 6-Gun Battery · XIV CORPS · HOOKER XX CORPS · A. McCook's Brigade · WILLIAMS'S DIVISION · Ruger · NEWTON (IV CORPS) · Union Pickets · Clear Cr. · Knipe · Robinson · GEARY'S DIVISION · Early's Cr. · WARD'S DIVISION · Bradley · Collier Rd. · Embry House · Reynolds · O'Neal · 33rd NJ · Kimball · Blake · Dr. Tanyard Branch · 4-Gun Battery · Scott · Featherston · Mt. Zion Church · WALTHALL · LORING · Vaughan · Carter · Walker (Maney) · WALKER · BATE · Strahl · Walker · MANEY (CHEATHAM) · Peachtree Rd. · N · FRENCH · STEWART · CLEBURNE · Key · Union · Confederate · Tanyard Branch · HARDEE · 0 1/4 1/2 Scale in Miles

BATTLE OF PEACHTREE CREEK

BATTLE OF PEACHTREE CREEK
Sherman's army advanced southward from the Chattahoochee in two groups. One, consisting of McPherson's Army of the Tennessee and Schofield's Army of the Ohio, marched to the Decatur area where it severed the Georgia Railroad and then turned west toward Atlanta. The other, Thomas's Army of the Cumberland (IV, XIV, and XX Corps), moved on Atlanta directly from the north. Hood, perceiving the wide gap between the Union forces, decided to exploit it. On the afternoon of July 20, Hardee's and Stewart's Corps assailed Thomas south of Peachtree Creek. Although the Confederates achieved some initial successes against the surprised Federals, their attack failed owing to poor coordination and inadequate strength.

McPherson and Schofield were moving toward Decatur, six miles east of Atlanta, and that Thomas was beginning to cross Peachtree Creek, five miles north of the city. Thus a wide gap existed between the two wings of the Union army. Hood at once decided to exploit it. At a late-night conference with his top generals he outlined a plan whereby, come tomorrow, Wheeler and Major General Benjamin F. Cheatham, who now headed Hood's former corps, would hold McPherson and Schofield in check while Hardee's and Stewart's Corps, under the operational command of Hardee, attacked Thomas's forces and drove them back to the banks of the Chattahoochee and Peachtree Creek at the point where the latter flowed into the former, trapping and destroying them. Then the following day the whole Confederate army would fall upon and crush McPherson and Schofield.

If successful, this plan would result in the greatest victory of the war. Unfortunately for the Confederates, it was based on the premise that McPherson and Schofield were advancing toward Decatur when in fact they were advancing from it and so were closer to Atlanta than Hood thought. Consequently, late on the morning of July 20 Wheeler, whose cavalry, fighting dismounted, opposed

MAJOR GENERAL BENJAMIN F. CHEATHAM

(USAMHI)

McPherson's advance along the Decatur-Atlanta road, had to call for help from Cheatham on his left. This caused Cheatham to shift to his right, which in turn obliged Hardee and Stewart to slide rightward also, thereby delaying their attack, which had been scheduled to begin at 1 P.M., by several hours.

Yet Hardee's and Stewart's re-deployment actually enhanced their prospects of success, for it placed most of Hardee's Corps beyond Thomas's left flank, which was held by Newton's division of the IV Corps—that corps' other two divisions were with Schofield—and put Stewart's Corps in position to assail the mainly unentrenched XX Corps instead of the strongly fortified XIV Corps, whose commander, General John Palmer, did not share the prevailing Union view that there was little or no danger of a Rebel attack north of Atlanta. In short, luck was with the Confederates; now all they needed was skill and determination.

Both of these qualities were conspic-uous for their absence in Hardee's assault. Bate's Division on the right literally got lost in the Peachtree Creek bottomlands

and thus did not engage the enemy, at least not seriously. In the center Major General W. H. T. Walker's Division deliv-ered a series of disjointed charges that Newton's troops, fighting from behind hastily improvised breastworks, easily repelled. And on Hardee's left Cheatham's Division, headed by Brigadier General George Maney, either did not attack at all or else went to ground on beholding Yankee trenches. With about 15,000 available troops, Hardee failed to dis-lodge, much less overpower, Newton's 3,200 men.

Stewart's attack, in contrast, was everything that Hardee's was not. Delivered with great ferocity by Loring's and Major General Edward Walthall's Divisions—Stewart had to hold back Major General Samuel French's Division and two brigades to cover his left flank—it nearly broke through the XX Corps, which was caught off guard and for the most part undeployed and unfortified. Loring's and Walthall's four brigades, how-ever, simply lacked the strength to sustain their advances against Hooker's nine brigades, which quickly rallied, and so they had to retreat. Undaunted, Stewart called on Hardee to renew the attack. Hardee concurred and ordered forward Cleburne's Division, hitherto held in reserve. But before Cleburne's crack troops could charge, Hardee received word from Hood that Wheeler urgently needed assistance, whereupon he can-celed their assault and sent them to the east side of Atlanta. So ended the Battle of Peachtree Creek. In it Hood, who lost at least 2,500 men, was foiled in his attempt to smash one-half of Sherman's army as a prelude to doing the same to the other half. Yet Sherman deserved no

credit for the Union victory, which cost nearly 2,000 casualties, most of them in the XX Corps. Because he was east of Atlanta, where he expected Hood to make a stand if he made one at all, he did not even know the battle had taken place until he received at midnight, six hours after it ended, a message from Thomas informing him of it. Moreover, during the height of the fighting along Peachtree Creek he sent an order to Thomas to occupy Atlanta, as there was no strong enemy force to oppose him. Finally, he did nothing to push forward McPherson, who, instead of sweeping aside Wheeler's cavalry with his 25,000 infantry, advanced with such cautious slowness on Atlanta that nightfall found him still more than a mile from the city. It was a case of Snake Creek Gap and Resaca all over again, and again Sherman must share the responsibility with McPherson.

The failure to drive Thomas into the Chattahoochee disappointed but did not discourage Hood: Sherman's army remained divided and hence vulnerable. Learning that McPherson's left flank was exposed—Sherman had sent off the caval-ry that should have been screening it to raid the railroad between Atlanta and Augusta, Georgia—Hood on the night of July 21 sent Hardee's Corps and Wheeler's cavalry swinging around that flank with orders to march to Decatur, then in the morning to pounce on McPherson from the rear, routing his forces and opening the way for Cheatham's troops to join with Hardee's and Wheeler's in doing the same to the rest of the Union army east of Atlanta. Meanwhile, Stewart, whose corps had fallen back to the city's north-side fortifications, would hold Thomas in check.

BATTLE OF ATLANTA

The night was hot, the roads dusty, and Hardee's soldiers already were half-exhausted from two days of fighting and marching, having spent July 21 holding the Federals east of Atlanta in check. Soon it became apparent that they could not hope to reach Decatur by morning. Hood thereupon, at Hardee's request, modified his plan: Wheeler would pro-

and that therefore the time had come to execute the strategy for taking it that he had outlined to Grant back in April: cut its railroad connections to the Confederacy. One of these, the line between Atlanta and Montgomery, already had been severed by a recent raid out of Tennessee into Alabama by Major General Lovell Rousseau's cavalry. Hence Sherman ordered McPherson to send Dodge's XVI Corps back to the Decatur area to wreak further destruction on the Georgia Railroad to Augusta, after which the Army of the Tennessee would swing north, then west of Atlanta to strike the Macon & Western Railroad, the breaking of which would completely isolate the city.

McPherson did not like this order and he went to Sherman to tell him why: large Confederate forces had been seen moving south and he feared an attack on his vulnerable left flank. Sherman, although he thought McPherson's concern was unwarranted, agreed to postpone the implementation of the order until 1 P.M. If by then the Rebels had not attacked, they never would.

The morning passed and no attack came. At noon Sherman sent a message to McPherson instructing him to direct

ceed to Decatur, where McPherson's wagon train reportedly was parked, but Hardee would attack as soon as he got beyond McPherson's flank.

Sherman, when informed early on the morning of July 22 that the enemy seemed to have withdrawn from in front of McPherson and Schofield, at once concluded that Hood was evacuating Atlanta and so instructed Schofield to occupy the city while the rest of the army gave pursuit. Then, on discovering that strong Confederate forces still occupied a line closer to Atlanta, Sherman decided that Hood intended to hold the place after all

40

Dodge to send Brigadier General John Fuller's division of the XVI Corps to Decatur to tear up tracks but to leave that corps' other division, Sweeny's, where it was, namely to the rear of McPherson's flank to which point it had marched during the morning after having been posted the previous evening on the right flank of the Army of the Tennessee to plug a gap between it and the XXIII Corps. McPherson did as Sherman directed. But before his dispatch could reach Dodge, an increasingly loud sound of firing came from the southeast.

It was Hardee, at long last launching his attack on the Union left and rear. Through no fault of his, its timing could not have been more unfavorable. Had it occurred either an hour sooner or an hour later, his two right divisions, Bate's and Walker's, would have met no opposition or only Sweeny's division. Instead, they encountered both Fuller and Sweeny. And to make matters worse, Bate's troops had to struggle across a swamp and Walker was killed by a Federal sniper before he could even deploy his division. As a result, the Confederate attack in this sector lacked cohesion and punch and soon was repulsed.

Likewise, Wheeler, although he took Decatur, failed to capture McPherson's wagon train, which escaped along with most of the Federals defending the place.

Cleburne's troops, on going into action, enjoyed better luck, for they happened to enter a wide gap between the right of XVI Corps and the left of the XVII Corps, which was at the south end of McPherson's line facing Atlanta. Furthermore, as they advanced McPherson himself, accompanied only by an orderly, came riding among them on his way to

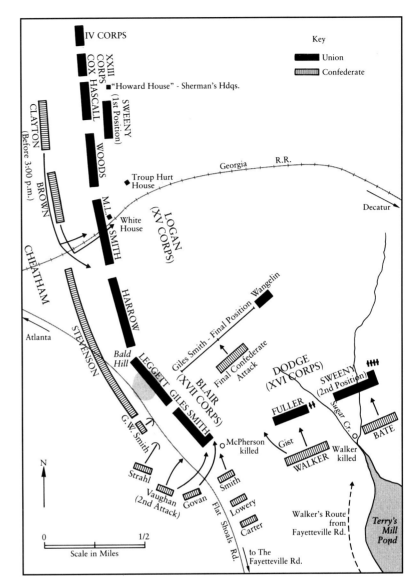

BATTLE OF THE BALD HILL, JULY 22
On the evening of July 21 Hardee's Corps, accompanied by Wheeler's cavalry, began marching southward with the object of swinging around the Union left flank to Decatur, where it would strike McPherson's forces, after which it was to join Cheatham's and Stewart's Corps in sweeping the rest of the Union army toward the Chattahoochee. When it became evident that Hardee could not reach Decatur by morning, Hood authorized him to attack on getting into the immediate rear of McPherson. Hardee could not accomplish this until after noon on July 22. His two right divisions, Walker's and Bate's, encountered Dodge's XVI Corps, which repulsed them. Only Cleburne's and a portion of Maney's division succeeded in penetrating a gap between the XVI and XVII Corps, in the process killing McPherson, and then bending back the XVII Corps until it occupied a line facing southward that was anchored on an elevation called the Bald Hill. Hood sought to transform this partial victory into a complete one by having Brown's and Clayton's Divisions attack the XV Corps. Two of Brown's brigades broke through along the Georgia Rairoad. But a counterattack by the XV Corps drove back Brown's troops and ended the Confederate threat in this sector. Even though Hardee continued to assail the Bald Hill until nightfall, he failed to seize it and the battle ended in another bloody defeat for Hood.

check the XVII Corps' situation after witnessing the XVI Corps beat back Bate's and Walker's attack. The Confederates yelled at him to surrender; instead he tried to escape and was shot dead from his horse. As he demonstrated on May 9 at Resaca, and two days earlier on the road to Atlanta, he was too lacking in aggressiveness to be a first-rate combat commander, but his caution served the Union cause well on July 22.

Pushing on, Cleburne's men struck the flank and rear of the XVII Corps while Cheatham's Division, still under Maney, assailed its front. These attacks, however, were uncoordinated, enabling the Federals to repel them by scrambling from one side of their entrenchments to the other. Not until after nearly two hours of bloody fighting did one of Cleburne's brigades join with one of Maney's to hit the Union line simultaneously in front and rear, causing the XVII Corps to fall back to a bald hill which, because of its height, dominated the battlefield and so was the key to it.

Hoping to help Hardee take the hill, Hood ordered Cheatham to attack the XV

Corps, which was astride the Georgia Railroad and to the right of the XVII Corps. Thanks to an inadequately defended railroad cut, two brigades from Brigadier General John C. Brown's Division (formerly Hindman's) penetrated the XV Corps' line and captured a four-gun battery. Their success, however, was short-lived. A Union counterattack, personally led by "Black Jack" Logan, who had assumed command of the Army of the Tennessee on McPherson's death, drove the Confederates back and restored the XV Corps' front. To the south, Hardee continued to assault the bald hill with both infantry and artillery until after it was dark, but to no avail as its defenders held on grimly. (The hill became known as Leggett's Hill after the commander of the XVII Corps division that defended it, Brigadier General Mortimer Leggett, who after the war purchased it.)

Night ended what would be called the Battle of Atlanta, the largest engagement of the Atlanta campaign, one that cost the Confederates about 5,500 casualties and the Federals nearly 4,000, a large proportion of whom were prisoners from the XVII Corps. Again Hood failed in an attempt to smash a wing of Sherman's army, a failure he attributed to Hardee for allegedly not carrying out orders to strike the Union rear but which in truth was caused by the semifortuitous presence of the XVI Corps in position to protect that rear and the steady fortitude of the soldiers of the XVII Corps. On the other hand, Sherman deserved little credit for the Federal victory, a victory which probably would have been a defeat had not McPherson persuaded Sherman to modify his orders regarding the XVI Corps. Moreover, during Cheatham's attack on

the XV Corps, Sherman rejected proposals from Schofield and Howard that their corps strike Cheatham's exposed left flank, a move that almost surely would have led to the rout of two-thirds of Hood's army.

BATTLE OF EZRA CHURCH

For the next four days both armies eyed each other like weary and wary wrestlers. During them Sherman placed Howard in command of the Army of the Tennessee, an act that so disgusted Hooker, who believed he was entitled to the post and who with good cause blamed Howard for his defeat at Chancellorsville, that he resigned as head of the XX Corps, which as a result came under the temporary command of Williams. Likewise, several command changes took place on the Confederate side, with the most important being the replacement of Cheatham as head of Hood's former corps by Lieutenant General Stephen D. Lee, a thirty-year-old

BATTLE SCENE FROM EZRA CHURCH.

(BL)

West Pointer who had been placed in charge of Mississippi and Alabama when Polk went to Georgia.

Early on the morning of July 27 Howard and the Army of the Tennessee began the movement that Sherman had planned to make before the July 22 battle—a swing around to the west side of Atlanta for the purpose of cutting the Macon railroad, Hood's sole remaining supply line. Although Sherman attempted to conceal the maneuver, Hood quickly discerned both it and its purpose. His reaction was to send, on the morning of July 28, Lee with two divisions of his corps (Brown's and Major General Henry D. Clayton's) out on the Lick Skillet road west of Atlanta with instructions to block Howard's southward advance while Stewart's Corps circled around by way of that road to attack Howard from the rear the following morning. In brief, Hood again sought to ambush and crush a major portion of Sherman's army, with the Army of the Tennessee once more his target.

Again he failed. Instead of taking up a defensive position covering the Lick Skillet road, the impulsive and over-aggressive Lee thought he saw an opportunity to hit Howard before his troops could entrench and so attacked near a small Methodist chapel called Ezra Church. Unfortunately for Lee—or rather for his soldiers—Howard, who equaled McPherson in prudence, had anticipated the Rebel onslaught despite assurances from Sherman that there was no danger of such and therefore had ordered his lead corps, the XV, to halt and fortify, which it did. What ensued was more a massacre than a battle. Logan's veterans mowed down the oncoming Confederates by the hundreds, stopping their assault cold. Not content with slaughtering his own troops, Lee thereupon asked Stewart, who had arrived on the scene with his corps, to throw Walthall's Division into the fray. Stewart did so and Walthall's men suffered the same fate as those of Lee's Corps. When the firing ceased, nearly 3,000 Confederates had been killed or wounded as opposed to one-fifth that number of Federals.

"How many men have you left?" a Union soldier called over to the "Rebs."

"Oh, enough for another killing or two," came the reply.

BROWN'S MILL AND SUNSHINE CHURCH

At the same time that Howard began his swing to the west of Atlanta, two of Sherman's cavalry divisions, McCook's and Stoneman's, headed south of the city. Their primary objective was to break the Macon railroad around Lovejoy's Station, following which Sherman had authorized Stoneman, should he believe it feasible, to go on to liberate the Union prisoners at Macon and Andersonville. On July 29 McCook reached the railroad at Lovejoy's and tore up two and a half miles of track but Stoneman did not join him there or even attempt to. Instead, as he probably intended from the first, he headed straight for Macon, after which he planned to go on to Andersonville in the hope of becoming the hero of the North by freeing the 30,000-plus Union captives incarcerated there.

As was invariably the case with him throughout the Civil War, Stoneman's aspirations far exceeded his accomplishments. At Macon on July 30 a makeshift force of home guards, militia, and convalescents repulsed his halfhearted attempt to take that town, and the next day pursuing Confederate cavalry forced him and seven hundred of his troopers to surrender near Sunshine Church. Joining them in captivity were hundreds of McCook's men, who had been overtaken and routed by Wheeler at Brown's Mill near Newnan on July 30 as they endeavored to make their way back to Union lines. Far from putting the Macon railroad out of action—the Confederates repaired the damage done to it at Lovejoy's—the McCook-Stoneman raid put out of action two of Sherman's four cavalry divisions.

SIEGE AND RAIDS (AUGUST 1–25)

Three times Hood had tried to strike a knockout blow against Sherman's army or at least cripple it so badly that it would have to retreat. Each time he had failed, in the process losing more men (11,000) than he could afford and intensifying the already strong reluctance of his remaining troops to charge an entrenched foe. Nevertheless, he stopped Sherman from taking Atlanta and, for the time being,

achieved the same sort of stalemate that Lee maintained at Richmond, where on July 30 his forces inflicted yet another bloody defeat on Grant in the Battle of the Crater. If Hood could manage to hold on to Atlanta until the fall elections in the North, there was an excellent chance that the Northern public, despairing of victory, would repudiate Lincoln and his policy of Union through war and turn to the Democrats with their promise of Union through peace. As July gave way to August, the Democrats confidently predicted such an outcome and many Republicans feared that they were right.

Fully aware that unless he won on the battlefront the war might be lost on the home front, Sherman spent the first three weeks of August trying to get Hood out of Atlanta and himself into it by some means other than assaulting its fortifications, which would have been suicidal given their enormous strength, or by undertaking another large-scale flanking maneuver, something he was reluctant to do as it would mean again leaving his

GENERAL
JOSEPH WHEELER

(LC)

THE PRISON CAMP
AT ANDERSONVILLE,
GEORGIA.

(LC)

STONEMAN'S RAID

By the last week of July 1864, Union forces had closed off three of the four railroads leading into Atlanta. Hood's army subsisted entirely on supplies coming in from the south, along the line of the Macon & Western Railroad.

With his army stretching in a wide crescent around the city, Sherman decided to snip this final corridor by sending out strong forces of cavalry from either tip of that crescent. The two would converge on the railroad at Lovejoy's Station, ripping up both the tracks and telegraph lines for several miles.

To lead the raid from his left, Sherman chose Major General George Stoneman, who was to take three small brigades of his own, numbering about 2,000 men, and a division of 3,000 more under Brigadier General Kenner Garrard. Garrard's troops had just returned from a raid to Covington, and Sherman cautioned Stoneman against taxing Garrard's worn-out horses. From his right, Sherman sent Brigadier General Edward McCook with his two-brigade division and a provisional division under Colonel Thomas Harrison. This wing totaled about 4,000 troopers, but Harrison's half of that force had just arrived from Alabama after an exhausting raid, and McCook was warned to use those troops only as a reserve. These assignments left Sherman with only one division of cavalry in his entire army.

Stoneman asked at the last moment for permission to attack Macon, releasing hundreds of imprisoned Union officers there, and to venture on to Andersonville from there, to free more than 30,000 men in that prison. Sherman granted him leave to try, but only after destroying both the railroad and the Confederate cavalry under Major General Joseph Wheeler.

Stoneman's hunger for the fame of liberating Andersonville led him to ignore both his orders and good judgment. His column left Decatur before dawn on July 27, and when he encountered Southern cavalry he left Garrard's division to contend with it. Wheeler drove Garrard back the next morning, leaving one brigade to monitor him while he sent the majority of his command after Stoneman, who had struck south for Macon. Meanwhile, Wheeler detached further troops to confront McCook's incursion, many miles to the west, where Brigadier General William Jackson stood alone with one intact brigade of horsemen.

McCook ripped up more than two miles of the Macon & Western rail lines, tore down several miles of telegraph wire, and pounced upon Confederate supply trains, burning hundreds of wagons full of provisions, killing the mules that pulled them, and capturing over 400 prisoners. Stoneman did not arrive to join him, so instead of finding reinforcements McCook found Wheeler's cavalry, which struck the rear of his command. McCook tried to escape by sweeping west, toward Newnan, but near there he was stopped by another of Wheeler's detached brigades. Wheeler soon hit McCook from behind again with another brigade, and the outnumbered Confederates convinced the Federals that they were hopelessly surrounded. McCook ordered the commanders of his own two brigades to release their captives and break out individually, while he held the enemy off with Harrison's division; eventually McCook cut his own way out, too, and the fragments of his command fled piecemeal toward the Chattahoochee, leaving behind hundreds of their comrades as prisoners, including both of McCook's brigade commanders and Colonel Harrison. The survivors started dribbling into Marietta on August 2, too exhausted for immediate service.

Stoneman reached Macon July 30, but found it defended at the Ocmulgee River by an inexperienced collection of Georgia Reserves, militia, and a number of citizen companies. He prodded at the town from the left bank of the Ocmulgee but failed to force a crossing. Stoneman turned his division to the south with the intention of riding to Florida, but reports of Southern cavalry threatening the river crossing in that direction convinced him to turn back to the north, for his starting place. On the morning of July 31, at Sunshine Church, he ran head-on into the three brigades Wheeler had sent after him. Like McCook, he supposed himself outnumbered, and also like McCook he ordered two of his brigadiers to break away while he remained with the third to cover their escape.

Stoneman and more than 700 of his men surrendered that afternoon, and within a day or two they occupied the very prisons they had intended to liberate.

Instead of closing off Hood's supply line, forcing the evacuation of Atlanta, and freeing tens of thousands of prisoners, Stoneman's raid had resulted in the virtual elimination of two Union cavalry divisions.

—William Marvel

46

railroad supply line, this time while deep in enemy territory.

First he made a second attempt to reach and block the Macon railroad by extending his right beyond the Confederate left. For this purpose he instructed Schofield to take command of Palmer's XIV Corps and with it and his own XXIII Corps advance south beyond the Lick Skillet road, where the Army of the Tennessee remained on the defensive. Putting Schofield over Palmer, however, invited trouble. Palmer, a political general who despised West Pointers, was tired of war, and wanted to go home, flatly refused to take orders from Schofield, declaring (quite correctly) that he was senior to him in rank. As a consequence, Schofield could employ only the XXIII Corps, and an assault by one of its brigades on August 6 against what he hoped would be a vulnerable point in the Confederate line along Utoy Creek was parried by Bate's Division. Meanwhile, Palmer, who had offered to do so several times previously during the campaign, resigned as commander of the XIV Corps, to be replaced by Jefferson C. Davis, a competent general but one whose main claim to fame was (and remains) the murdering of a fellow Federal general in Louisville in 1862.

Next Sherman endeavored, as he put it in a telegram to Halleck, to "make the inside of Atlanta too hot to be endured." Starting on August 9 his artillery rained shells and solid shot on the city both day and night. The bombardment did considerable damage to buildings in the northern part, killed and injured a hundred or so civilians, among them women and children, but achieved no military effect whatsoever. Indeed, soon the townspeople, many of whom constructed dugouts in their backyards, came to regard the Yankee barrages as more a nuisance than a serious danger.

Sherman, who even as he ordered the bombardment admitted that "I am too impatient for a siege," thereupon decided that he had to make another big flanking move after all. But before this could get under way, Wheeler with five to six thousand of his best cavalry descended upon the Western & Atlantic Railroad north of the Chattahoochee, sent there by Hood in an effort to force Sherman to retreat by destroying his supply line. For several days during mid-August Sherman issued a stream of orders designed to counter Wheeler's raid while awaiting reliable word as to its outcome. When that word came, he felt most relieved: although Wheeler captured a small garrison and tore up some track near Dalton and a few other places, he did no damage to the railroad that could not be (and was) rapidly repaired. Better still, from Sherman's standpoint, he continued

northward into East Tennessee, in effect taking his cavalry out of the campaign.

Realizing this, Sherman made another attempt to break Hood's supply line with his own cavalry (what was left of it). On his orders Brigadier General Judson Kilpatrick with 4,700 troopers struck the Macon railroad at Jonesboro, fifteen miles due south of Atlanta, on the evening of August 19, then on the following day endeavored to do the same at Lovejoy's Station, only to be repulsed by two brigades of Jackson's cavalry supported by infantry. Returning to Union lines on August 22, Kilpatrick boasted to Sherman that it would take the enemy ten days to repair the damage he had inflicted on the railroad.

Sherman doubted this and with good reason, for already trains were entering Atlanta, trains that could only be coming from Macon. Hence on the night of August 22 he telegraphed Halleck that although he had hoped that Kilpatrick's raid would spare him the need to make "a long, hazardous flank march," he would have to "swing across" the Macon railroad "in force to make the matter certain."

During the nights of August 25 and 26 the Union army pulled out of its trenches and began marching in a great arc to the west and south of Atlanta,

leaving behind only the XX Corps to guard the rebuilt railroad bridge over the Chattahoochee. From Sherman down to the drummer boys, the Federals felt that the final, decisive act of the campaign had begun.

"ATLANTA IS OURS"

Confederate pickets quickly discovered and reported that the Federals had vacated their trenches. At first Hood thought that this might mean that Sherman was retreating, as he had received greatly exaggerated claims of success from Wheeler and both spies and civilians testified that the Yankees were short of food. Soon, however, he ascertained that except for the XX Corps all of the Union army was to the southwest of Atlanta and that its probable objective was the Macon railroad. But exactly where on that railroad would Sherman strike? Until Hood knew that—and also could be sure that Sherman was not merely feinting toward the railroad before assaulting Atlanta on its weakly fortified south side—all Hood could do was what he did do: wait for reliable intelligence as to Sherman's movements and intentions.

That came on the evening of August 30 in the form of cavalry reports to the effect that Howard's Army of the Tennessee was approaching Jonesboro. At once Hood ordered Hardee to march his and Lee's corps to that town and in the morning drive Howard's forces into the Flint River, following which Lee would return to Atlanta and join Stewart in attacking the rest of Sherman's army from the north while Hardee assailed it from the south. Once more Hood, not content

simply to parry one of Sherman's thrusts, sought to smash him.

As before, he failed. Although Hardee's Corps, under the acting command of Cleburne, reached Jonesboro on the morning of August 31, all of Lee's Corps, which had a longer march to make, did not arrive there until early afternoon. As a result Hardee was unable to deliver his attack until about 3:30 P.M. By then Howard, whose 20,000 troops at least equaled in number Hardee's effective force, had had ample time to fortify along a line of ridges west of Jonesboro. Only by some military miracle could the Confederates have carried the Union position, and no such miracle occurred. Instead, the Federals, with Logan's XV Corps doing most of the fighting, easily repulsed the ill-coordinated and halfhearted Rebel assaults, inflicting approximately 2,200 casualties, 1,400 of them in Lee's Corps, while suffering a mere 172 themselves. It was a more one-sided slaughter than even Ezra Church had been and the only thing that prevented it from being worse was the refusal of many Confederate units to engage the enemy or to press forward once they came under fire.

Shortly after midnight a courier brought Hood word of Hardee's defeat. It had to come by courier because, even as Hardee vainly endeavored to drive Howard's forces away from the Macon railroad, portions of the XXIII, IV, and XIV Corps reached that railroad north of Jonesboro and south of Rough and Ready, whereupon they cut the telegraph wire to Atlanta. Thus, when Hood read Hardee's message, he realized that there was no possibility of regaining control of the railroad and that the only choice left him

From Sherman down to the drummer boys, the Federals felt that the final, decisive act of the campaign had begun.

The Citizens' War: Inside Atlanta during the siege

Just before noon on Wednesday, July 20, 1864, a family of Southern refugees composed of a father, mother, and a little girl stood at the corner of East Ellis Street and Ivy Street--now known as Peachtree Center Avenue. To the east, a Federal artillery crew loaded a shell into their 20-pounder Parrott rifle and pulled the lanyard, sending the projectile hurtling through the sweltering summer air. The shell exploded right over the refugee family, and when the smoke cleared the stunned parents saw their little girl lying dead in the dusty street. The siege of Atlanta had claimed its first noncombatant victim.

Atlanta's civilians shared the danger and misery of their defenders for more than six weeks. Some citizens did leave, especially in the first few days of the siege, including the newspaper publishers and postal officials, but many stayed or returned shortly afterward when Sherman's troops failed to take the city.

Union shells rained on the city until it surrendered, forty-four days later, but at first the bombardment was so indolent that residents found little cause to avoid it beyond giving a wide berth to prominent targets like railroad landmarks and tall buildings. On July 23 a store owner named S. P. Richards recorded that a shell landing near his home threw dirt in his open windows, and that night he positioned his family's beds behind the shelter of his chimney, but he noted that he saw no more damage done that night.

The pace of the barrage

was to evacuate Atlanta. This he ordered done as soon as it became dark on September 1. Meanwhile, Lee's Corps, as previously directed, would return to Atlanta to guard against a Federal thrust from the south, and Hardee was to hold on at Jonesboro so as to cover the retreat of the rest of the Confederate army southward.

Sherman's orders for September 1 called for the IV Corps, followed by the XXIII Corps, to move down the railroad, destroying the track as it went, until it reached the Jonesboro area where it was to join the XIV Corps in an attack on Hardee's forces, which Sherman thought still included Lee's Corps despite having been notified to the contrary by Thomas. Not until the early afternoon of September 1 did Sherman realize that Thomas's information was correct and that only Hardee's Corps faced him at Jonesboro. He then directed Major General David S. Stanley, who had replaced Howard as commander of the IV Corps, to stop tearing up rails and hasten to assist the XIV Corps in attacking what Sherman believed to be Hardee's exposed right flank north of increased as the Federals seemed to grow impatient. Citizens frequently retreated to their cellars, or dug makeshift bunkers in their yards, to avoid the sudden flurries of shells. One little girl who kept a diary wrote of spending the entire day of August 9 in her family's cellar because the shells were dropping so closely around her house.

August 9 proved to he the bloodiest day of the siege for the citizens of Atlanta. One shell exploded in a house at the corner of Elliott and Rhodes streets, instantly killing both J. H. Warner, superintendent of the city gas company, and his six-year-old daughter; a woman ironing clothing in a house on Pryor Street was killed by another shell; a free black barber named, ironically, Solomon Luckie, was wounded in the leg by a shell fragment while standing at the corner of Whitehall and Alabama streets and died in spite of an amputation; a young woman walking near the railroad depot was struck in the back by a piece of shell and killed; a Confederate officer saying good-bye to a woman in her front yard was killed, as was her young son, by a single shell.

A few days afterward, S. P. Richards was inspecting the condition of his store when a shell crashed through the rooms above him, covering him in dust.

"It is like living in the midst of a pestilence," Richards wrote. "No one can tell but he may be the next victim."

The fourth week of August began with another heavy barrage, but after three days the shelling subsided as Union troops swept south of Atlanta. August 25 began a week of ominous silence: the calm before the storm. Eight days later, the city fell.

From the outset, Atlanta was crowded with Confederate troops, both on duty and off. On the night of July 21 the store owned by S. P. Richards was broken into by Southern cavalrymen who stole all his merchandise and what little cash he had remaining in the till. Wagons and troops jammed the streets as the Army of Tennessee passed through the city, and male citizens were required to take arms and perform police duty. Wounded men poured into Atlanta, wearing both blue and gray: the fairgrounds became one vast hospital for Confederate casualties, while Union wounded were cared for in the southeastern quadrant of town. Forage for livestock ran out altogether, so horses and cattle subsisted almost entirely on what they could graze from patches of grass.

Martial law ruled the city, and civilians going about their business had to show passes. That ended with the beginning of September, though: when Federal troops gained control of the last rail line into the city, the Confederate army evacuated. Through the night of September 1 and the morning of September 2 throngs of deserters, stragglers, abandoned slaves, and desperate refugees filled the streets, looting empty stores and homes. Residents huddled in their homes, expecting to see their city pillaged either by the mob or by the Yankees. With no other recourse, Mayor James Calhoun rode out Marietta Street that morning and surrendered his city, asking the protection of Union troops for private property and the civilian population.

That protection was granted, but only for a few days. On September 8 General Sherman issued Order No. 67, requiring that all civilians not connected with the Union army depart the city. After a series of indignant, unavailing protests from the Confederates the exodus began, and over ten days virtually all the civilian citizens were evacuated.

—William Marvel

CAPTURED CONFEDERATES ARE LED TO PRISON CAMP AFTER THE BATTLE OF JONESBORO.

(FRANK AND MARIE WOOD PRINT COLLECTION)

Jonesboro. If Hardee could be crushed—and Sherman was confident that he would be—then Hood either would have to abandon Atlanta or else stay there until starvation forced him to surrender the city and what was left of his army. Or so Sherman calculated; evidently it did not occur to him that with his only supply line, the Macon railroad, in Union possession, Hood's sole rational alternative was to do what in fact he was preparing to do —leave Atlanta as soon as safely possible.

Starting at 4 P.M., just as the van of the IV Corps came up, the XIV Corps

made a series of assaults on Hardee's right flank. By stripping his front facing Howard's Army of the Tennessee, which Sherman had directed to "demonstrate" but which did not even do that, Hardee was able to reinforce his right sufficiently to beat back the initial attacks. But then three XIV Corps brigades managed to carry a weak point on the Confederate line, swamping the Arkansas brigade of Cleburne's Division, most of whose men held their ground until killed or physically overpowered. It was the first and only successful large-scale frontal attack of the entire campaign. Yet Hardee, by bringing up still more troops from his center and left, sealed off the Union breakthrough and also prevented the IV Corps from getting into his rear until night put an end to the battle. Hardee thereupon withdrew his forces from their trenches and headed south toward Lovejoy's Station, having conducted one of the finest defensive stands of the war—thanks in large part to Sherman, who botched an opportunity to demolish Hardee's Corps and so wreck Hood's army.

While Hardee's men marched south,

so did the troops of Stewart, Lee, and the Georgia militia as they left Atlanta via the McDonough road. Before departing the Confederates set fire to boxcars filled with ammunition, setting off tremendous explosions that leveled nearby buildings, among them a rolling mill, and which could be heard all the way to Jonesboro. Sherman, unsure as to what this meant, asked a local farmer who told him that it sounded like a battle. Agreeing, Sherman concluded that Hood remained in Atlanta and probably was engaging Union forces south of the city. Sherman also believed that Hardee still was at Jonesboro, declaring that it would be impossible for him to slip away undetected.

In the morning, on discovering that Hardee had done precisely that, Sherman gave belated pursuit. North of Lovejoy's Station he came upon Hardee's forces strongly entrenched—so strongly that he decided not to attack and instead await definite word as to the situation in and around Atlanta. Early on the morning of September 3 a dispatch arrived from Major General Henry B. Slocum, who recently had taken command of the XX Corps, that his troops had occupied the city yesterday. That night a telegram from Sherman reached the War Department in Washington. It read: "Atlanta is ours, and fairly won." Two days later, by which time all of Hood's army had reassembled at Lovejoy's, the Union troops, as soon as it was dark, left their trenches and began marching north toward Atlanta. The campaign had ended.

POST-MORTEM

On August 23, the day after Sherman definitely decided to swing the bulk of his army to the south of Atlanta, Lincoln had the members of his cabinet sign, unseen, a memorandum stating that "it seems exceedingly probable that this Administration will not be reelected. Then it will be my duty to so cooperate with the President-elect, as to save the Union between the election and the inauguration; as he will have secured his election on such ground that he cannot possibly save it afterward."

On August 31, even as Sherman's army repulsed Hardee's attack at Jonesboro and reached the Macon railroad, the Democratic national convention, meeting in Chicago, nominated General George B. McClellan for president on a platform that declared the war a failure and called for "a cessation of hostilities, with a view to an ultimate convention of the States or other peaceable means, to the end that at the earliest practicable moment peace may be restored on the basis of the Federal Union of the States."

Thus as August drew to an end both Lincoln and the Democrats expected that a war-weary North, despairing of victory, would elect a president committed to restoring the Union by means of peace rather than force. And the same expectation prevailed in the South, where on August 20 the *Richmond Sentinel*, which reflected the views of Jefferson Davis, predicted that if the Confederate armies continued to hold Grant and Sherman at bay for just six more weeks, "we are almost sure to be in much better condition to treat for peace than we are now," for the North no longer would be willing and therefore able to go on with the war.

Sherman's capture of Atlanta immediately and decisively reversed the mood of the North and the expectations of Lincoln, the Democrats, and the South. To the majority of Northerners it meant that the war was being won and so should be continued until the Union was restored and slavery, the thing that had caused the war, was totally eradicated. Likewise, Lincoln's pessimism about his election prospects, which other Republican leaders shared, turned to optimism, an optimism

that proved fully justified when he was reelected by a landslide majority. On the other hand, the fall of Atlanta wrecked both the Democratic platform and McClellan's candidacy. And in the South it became clear to all except the most fanatical that the North would go on with the war until its superior might prevailed, as it did, even though the dwindling remnants of the Confederate army struggled on desperately for six more months before Lee mounted the steps of the McLean house at Appomattox Court House.

Johnston blamed Davis and Hood for the loss of Atlanta and they in turn blamed Johnston. Actually all three of

UNION SOLDIERS PHOTOGRAPHED IN A FORT NEAR ATLANTA.

(LC)

53

them shared the responsibility. Davis badly overestimated the military potential of the Army of Tennessee and underestimated the power of the Federal forces arrayed against it. Yet he furnished Johnston with more troops than Lee had to oppose Grant (about 75,000, whereas Lee had about 60,000); he retained Johnston in command until it became manifest that he could not be relied on to make a whole-hearted effort to defend Atlanta, the sole thing Davis asked of him; and he was justified in not sacrificing Mississippi and Alabama by sending Forrest to attack Sherman's supply line, for not only would this have deprived the Army of Tennessee of its logistical base, it also probably would not have achieved any decisive result: not once during the Civil War did cavalry raids on railroads

turn back the advance of a major army and it is extremely doubtful that Forrest, military genius that he was, could have provided an exception.

Johnston, as he was throughout his Civil War career, was more concerned during the Atlanta campaign with avoiding defeat than gaining victory. For this reason, and because of his inferior numbers, he for the most part adhered strictly to the defensive. Later he claimed that by so doing he preserved the strength of his forces while wearing down that of Sherman's to a point where he could and would have, when the Federals neared Atlanta, carried out a successful offensive had he not been removed from command. In truth, however, the Confederate army during May, June, and early July suffered a higher percentage of loss from all causes (killed, wounded, sick, captured, and desertion) than did the Union army, with the result that Sherman was proportionately stronger when he crossed the Chattahoochee than he was when he advanced from the Etowah. Furthermore, Johnston's postwar assertions that he could have, had he remained in command, held Atlanta "forever" or "indefinitely" (whatever that means) are more than dubious, they are fatuous. If Johnston could not effectively counter Sherman's flanking maneuvers in the mountains of northern Georgia, what good reason is there for believing he would have done so in the relatively flat terrain around Atlanta? None. The most likely outcome of Johnston having remained in command is that Sherman would have entered Atlanta in late July instead of early September.

Hood attempted to do what Davis wanted done: shatter Sherman's army or

THE CYCLORAMA

The hour of 4:30 on the afternoon of Friday, July 22, 1864, is forever preserved on the half-acre canvas of the Atlanta Cyclorama at Grant Park, on Boulevard in southeastern Atlanta. Even more impressive than the better-known Gettysburg Cyclorama, which depicts the acme of Pickett's Charge, this magnificent rendering of the Battle of Atlanta stands fifty feet tall inside a marble pantheon not far from the actual scenes portrayed.

The painting was begun in Milwaukee two decades after the battle and was the collective creation of ten German artists who labored for a year and a half to include every possible detail of the action. The best-recognized feature of the painting is the brick, hip-roofed Troup Hurt house, an unfinished structure standing near the Georgia Railroad—a little nearer in the painting than it was actually situated, in fact. Around the house swarm Alabama and South Carolina troops belonging to the brigade of Brigadier General Arthur Manigault, engaged with Midwesterners (mostly from Illinois and Ohio) under Brigadier General Joseph Lightburn. To the right of this, the Mississippians of Colonel Jacob Sharp's brigade can be seen moving against the newly arrived brigade of Colonel Augustus Mersy, whose men also hailed from Illinois and Ohio. Over the carnage soars an eagle, said to represent "Old Abe," the mascot of the 8th Wisconsin Volunteers, which took flight whenever its regiment went into action; if that is the intention, the bird represents a flaw in the painting's accuracy, for Old Abe and the 8th Wisconsin were hundreds of miles to the west, in Mississippi, during the Battle of Atlanta.

Lightburn's Federals fell back in disorder when Manigault's and Sharp's Confederates pierced their line: the Southerners poured through, overrunning two Illinois batteries and rolling up the Union trenches. They threatened to force the Federal XV Corps backward onto the rear of the XVI and XVII Corps, which were already under attack from the front by William Hardee's corps, but General Sherman ordered up additional artillery and John Logan shifted Mersy's fresh brigade from the Union left to help patch the breach. With rallied troops of Lightburn's, Mersy's brigade swept forward to regain their lost works.

It is at this juncture that the action of the cyclorama is frozen. Battery horses lie dead or dying between the lines, killed so the Confederates could not carry away the artillery pieces they had overrun; Southern sharpshooters have taken refuge in the brick house; a cleated tree that served as an impromptu Union signal tower stands abandoned; an ambulance carries away the grievously wounded Union general, Manning Force, who survived a hideous wound to the upper part of his face; soldiers fight hand-to-hand for the entrenchments.

Originally housed under a dome on Edgewood Avenue more than a century ago, the cyclorama was later moved to Grant Park, where it was extensively renovated in the early 1980s.

—William Marvel

A SMALL PORTION OF THE CYCLORAMA.

(NPS)

at least damage it so badly that it would be compelled to retreat. Obviously he failed. Although excellent in concept, his battle plans were unrealistic in practice, for they required too few troops to do too much without a sufficient margin for time and error. Consequently, it might have been better if Hood, while fighting aggressively, had sought less ambitious objectives that were more suited to the limited offensive capability of his army, with the purpose of throwing Sherman off balance, putting him on the defensive, and thus denying him Atlanta as long as

bloody offensive battles designed to knock out the enemy with one mighty blow but instead employing flanking moves to compel the Confederates to abandon one strong position after another and finally Atlanta itself. His sole major failure, one stemming from his concept of warfare and a fixation with capturing Atlanta to the near exclusion of all other objectives, was not to take advantage of the numerous opportunities he had to destroy the opposing army in Georgia or mangle it so badly as to render it strategically impotent. As a consequence, Hood's forces, although badly battered, remained a source of danger and trouble until Thomas finally smashed them at the Battle of Nashville in December 1864.

possible—mayhap until after the North's presidential election. But Hood could not have done this and still be Hood; he would have had to been Lee. And that he was not, even though he tried his best to be.

On the Union side the campaign for Atlanta was, as Grant declared in a telegram of congratulations to Sherman, "the most gigantic undertaking given to any general in the war." Sherman owed his success mainly to Confederate mistakes, to not making any irreparable blunders of his own, and above all to the superior power and high quality of his army, which he maintained by not, like Grant in Virginia, repeatedly engaging in

But if Sherman failed to do as much as he could and should have done, he accomplished what he set out to do and had to do: take Atlanta. And in doing that he guaranteed the North's victory by depriving the South of its last chance of winning—of winning by not losing.

On January 1, 1864, Mary Chesnut of South Carolina had written in her diary: "God help my country!" Nine months later, on learning of Atlanta's fall, she wrote: "No hope." Those two words said it all.